S0-BPP-133

ADHD: Helping Parents Help Their Children

ADHD: Helping Parents Help Their Children

Edward H. Jacobs, Ph.D.

JASON ARONSON INC.
Northvale, New Jersey
London

The people and situations described herein are based on real people and situations or composites of real people and situations that have been modified to protect the identities of the individuals.

This book was set in 11 pt. Janson by Pageworks of Old Saybrook and Lyme, CT and printed and bound by Book-mart Press, Inc. of North Bergen, NJ.

10 9 8 7 6 5 4 3 2 1

Library of Congress Cataloging-in-Publication Data

Jacobs, Edward H.
ADHD : helping parents help their children / Edward H. Jacobs.
p. cm.
Includes bibliographical references and index.
ISBN 0-7657-0273-8
1. Attention-deficit-disordered children—Family relationships. 2. Attention-deficit hyperactivity disorder—Treatment. I. Title.
RJ506.H9 J328 2000
618.92'8589—dc21 00-020328

Printed in the United States of America on acid-free paper. For information and catalog write to Jason Aronson Inc., 230 Livingston Street, Northvale, NJ 07647-1726, or visit our website: www.aronson.com

This work is dedicated lovingly to my wife,
best friend, and best colleague

Vicki Touster Jacobs, MSW

and to her creators

Gloria and Ted Touster

❖ ❖ ❖

Contents

❖ ❖ ❖

Acknowledgments

My greatest gratitude and appreciation for making this book a reality goes to my wife, Vicki T. Jacobs, MSW, who in one way or another has been involved in every idea presented in these pages. From her I have also gained the time and the encouragement to write, in effect beginning a second career within our already busy lives.

I extend my heartfelt thanks to my children, Rebecca and Joshua, who, at their young ages, have shared my wonder at creating a book.

I appreciate the thoughtful comments of my brother, David Jacobs, and my sister, Dale Jacobs, which enabled me to make the book more practical and complete.

I have been blessed with more than one person's fair share of talented, respectful, intelligent, ethical and, most of all, patient, teachers and supervisors at all levels of my education, training, and career. I strive daily to be worthy of their investment.

I greatly appreciate the hard work, care, and diplomacy that go into editing a book, I am grateful to my editors, Judy Cohen and David Kaplan, for helping me communicate more effectively, to Dr. Michael Moskowitz, for signing on to the idea of the book, and to Anne Marie Dooley and Dr. Jason Aronson, for sharpening the focus of the original manuscript.

Finally, I am humbled by the courage shown by the parents of my young patients. Every day, as they live their lives, they somehow find the energy for the struggle to make their children's lives better and to reach beyond their pain and self-doubt to be the best parents that they are capable of being. It is that courage and persistence that make my work worthwhile.

❖ ❖ ❖

Introduction

HOW TO USE THIS GUIDEBOOK

In my twenty-five years of working with children with attention-deficit/hyperactivity disorder (ADHD) and their families, I have found no simple solutions. There are things that tend to work and things that don't, but, as a clinician, trying to make something work with one child or family that has worked with others in the past is always an endeavor fraught with uncertainty. The application of every therapeutic approach or technique is complicated by the individuality of the child; the peculiarities of the family system in which the child lives; the complexities, the strengths, and the weaknesses of the institutions in which the child functions; and the skill, experience, training, biases, and quirks of the clinician doing the therapy.

I have seen very good ideas and very good techniques backfire by my failure to take into account the whole picture, by my inability to listen to what the client needed, or by my solutions being inflexible. While it might be comforting to attribute treatment failures to the clients, it behooves clinicians to look within to find what will make them better at providing services.

Therapists who are to work effectively with children who have ADHD must have special skills. They must have a thorough understanding of the diagnostic criteria, as well as of both the utility and the confusion inherent in these criteria. They should be able to evaluate research well enough to know how useful, practical, or generalizable its findings are. They must also have a solid knowledge of other diagnoses that might look like ADHD or coexist with it, such as bipolar disorder, dysthymic disorder, anxiety disorder, learning disabilities, oppositional defiant disorder, conduct disorder, and pervasive developmental disorders.

Therapists must be knowledgeable about normality and pathology in child development, the nature and dynamics of family systems, the functioning of community institutions such as schools, as well as good parenting skills and how to impart them to struggling parents. It is to this last "must" that this guidebook is dedicated, while keeping in mind that the integration of all these abilities and skills is essential in being a good ADHD therapist. Helping parents develop better parenting skills is much more complicated than it might seem.

Those clinicians who work with parents realize that things rarely go smoothly. Because we are armed with very useful techniques and brimming with enthusiasm, our work should be easy, if only parents would just accept our good sense and do what we recommend. But working with parents is complicated. We cannot approach parenting as a generic activity and try to avoid or minimize the very real differences that often exist between mothers and fathers. We should think in terms of "mothering" and "fathering" rather than the more generic term "parenting."

This guidebook is intended to help clinicians understand these differences, to communicate this understanding and appreciation to parents, and to help parents make creative use of their differences and conflicts in order for them to work together to be more effective parents to their children with ADHD. Just as special skills are needed by clinicians working with children and families coping with ADHD, special skills are needed to parent the ADHD child. This guidebook is also intended to help clinicians enable parents to develop those skills and address the different needs and perspectives of mothers and fathers that can create confusion, disagreement, misunderstanding, and conflict. These differences can also be used to find creative ways to parent the ADHD child cooperatively. This guidebook, then, is designed to help clinicians effectively help parents of ADHD children to acquire skills that will help their children, to help these parents become more skilled at helping themselves and helping their spouses or ex-spouses, to help mothers and fathers appreciate what is unique to each of their perspectives and understand what is unique to their spouse's or ex-spouse's perspective, and to help them find creative ways to use this knowledge to work together for the benefit of their ADHD child.

This guidebook enables therapists to help parents use the wisdom they already have to become more effective and satisfied in their parenting. Despite the powerful feelings of frustration and failure that the parents are experiencing, they are doing some things right, even if they are too overwhelmed to be aware of it.

The exercises in this book enable therapists to help parents identify their strengths and their needs, set goals for themselves, and learn ways to help their children. The information is intended not to specifically address the needs of any individual child, but rather to help parents tailor their mothering and fathering to help *their* child. It will help them to build on what they know about themselves and their children to create change in their families and to help their children become more successful at home, at school, and with friends.

It is not enough to teach parents to understand the disorder, to train parents in effective behavior management techniques, and to coach children in self-monitoring, self-soothing, and self-control techniques. As important as these factors are, they all fall apart if the parents are unable to work together as a team. What is important in this context is an appreciation of gender differences in parenting. Grappling with these differences is essential for effective parenting to take place.

My family therapy professor at Temple University, Dr. James Framo, said: "The most important gift that parents can give their children is a good marriage." It is that gift that I want us to help parents of ADHD children to give to their children. If ADHD children are to have a good start in life, are to overcome the challenges with which they have to begin life, are to learn to channel their behavior into productive and self-fulfilling pursuits, and are to benefit from all the techniques that we have to offer them, this gift is indispensable to their success.

There are several forms to be filled out in this book. Clinicians may use them as they appear in the book, copy them, or modify them. This book can be used as a resource with or without the forms. I developed the forms to concretize some of the work that I do and the thinking and problem solving I engage in with parents. The use of concrete exercises, forms, and techniques makes it easier to think about how to implement the learning that we want to impart to parents, and to convey information and skills. Much of this teaching can be done in the context of the clinician's relationship with parents and through the parents' relationship with one another. This guidebook/workbook format presents a way of thinking about these issues and facilitates productive clinical work. Parents can do these exercises alone or together. Clinicians can experiment with different approaches and find the way that works best. Clinicians should review the guidebook in full before jumping into the exercises to get an overview of what the book offers and to find the exercises that are most relevant to their practice. This book can also be used directly by parents on their own.

An important component of the clinician's work is to help the parents train themselves to provide frequent praise for the child when he is acting in an appropriate way. Quietly playing with his toys, cooperating with his siblings, or waiting his turn to speak are behaviors that are worthy of positive feedback. Clinicians must also help parents be generous in praising themselves and each other for taking on this task of learning more about themselves and working to improve their relationship with their child and with each other. They, too, need frequent positive feedback for their honesty, their self-examination, their persistence, and their desire to have the best possible relationship with their child.

AN OUTLINE OF THE GUIDEBOOK

Chapter 1 addresses the nature of the therapeutic relationship in working with parents of children with ADHD. With all the books about ADHD and about techniques and methods that are effective, there is insufficient attention paid to the nature of the therapeutic relationship that facilitates this work. After all, even with the scientific and technical knowledge necessary to do this work effectively, we are not merely technicians, we are clinicians. The manner in which we impart the knowledge that we have is as important as the knowledge itself. The process is as vital as the content. Without appropriate attention to this relationship, our knowledge and wisdom might not do much good.

There used to be much more attention paid to the relationship in therapy than there seems to be today. As the science and technology of human behavior have advanced, and as providers have been held more accountable for results in measurable, behavioral terms, the techniques of psychotherapy have become more of the focus of our work. What risks being lost is the practice of being thoughtful about the process of therapy.

Chapter 1 discusses how active and directive therapists should be, what the implications are of the therapist's giving advice to parents, and how the therapist should weigh the benefits and risks of facilitating conflict resolution between parents versus jumping in with information. All of these concerns have impact on the time-honored notion of therapeutic neutrality. Is this concept relevant in this type of work? How can the therapist deal with challenges to his or her authority from parents, and through what lens should the therapist view such behavior? What constitutes acting out by the parents, and how can the therapist deal with this productively? What are the pros and cons of therapist self-disclosure, which also impacts on transferential issues in the therapist's relationship with the parents? Related to this matter is the notion that this type of work can provide a corrective emotional experience for the parents, providing parenting for the parents to help them be more effective. In this type of work, the therapist takes on various roles. How do these roles affect the therapist's functioning and the goals of therapy? I consider the question of the length of treatment and the selection of the appropriate therapeutic modality—whether one should work with the parents, the child, the family, and/or the school, and helping the parents to be advocates for their child.

Chapter 2 discusses how to explain the nature of ADHD to parents. It is a challenge to help the parents understand this disorder in a way that does not oversimplify it or overwhelm them. The parents need not only information but also help in coping with their emotional reactions. I review the major symptoms and the diagnostic criteria of ADHD in simple terms and explain the meaning of the diagnosis. I also explain related symptoms and problems, such as deficits in rule-governed behavior, reinforcement sensitivity, executive functions, the ability to anticipate the future, social and communication skills, memory, response speed, self-esteem, emotional regulation, and cooperative behavior.

Chapter 3 discusses how to help parents understand the nature of the diagnostic process and the difficulties of making an accurate diagnosis of ADHD. The diagnosis of ADHD is confusing for parents. Compounding this confusion is the emotional stress of hearing that your child might have a lifelong condition. This chapter examines the challenges of understanding the established diagnostic criteria and the complications of differentiating ADHD from related or coexisting disorders.

Chapter 4 explores the assessment process for parents and discusses the central role that parents play in identifying the child's problem. It helps them look at the child's behavior historically, noting the persistence of certain problems over time and noting the evidence of such problems. I discuss the importance of early identification of the disorder. Several factors confuse and complicate the assessment process. These factors, which are created by the nature of ADHD itself and by the process that we as professionals engage in, are examined. I ask parents to look at how active their participation in the assessment process is, and give them tools to evaluate and monitor that participation with the school and with their child's physician. I then give some information about psychological testing.

Chapter 5 discusses helping the parents identify the problems that their child has that are associated with ADHD. I then provide exercises that can help parents set and prioritize goals in order to improve their child's behavior and to improve their own behavior in relation to their child. Here, the parents get to examine in some detail their own strengths and weaknesses as parents and how they handle problem situations, and to work toward changes in their own behavior. This chapter helps parents develop an action plan to monitor the changes they wish to make.

Chapter 6 discusses how the therapist explores with parents the different styles of authority and related disciplinary techniques. Parents might not realize that there is more than one way to be an effective authority, and that the type of authority affects the struggles they have with their children. Parents are guided to examine the types of discipline they use and how effective these methods are. "Time-out" is explored in some detail, with an attempt to differentiate the productive use of time-out from the counterproductive. How and why to use praise is also discussed. I review some of the differences between mothers and fathers that I have found repeatedly cause conflicts but can be employed creatively to make parents even more effective. Finally, this chapter addresses how to respond to children who repeatedly demand explanations, argue like lawyers, behave disrespectfully, and engage parents in control struggles.

Chapter 7 discusses specific skills that parents can teach their ADHD child, such as how to communicate more effectively. The chapter also presents different options for employing behavior management systems, depending on the concerns of the parent, the home situation, and the behavior of the child. Systems and charts are explained. The chapter then discusses the issue of developing better social skills in the child by the use of the Social Skills Report Card technique. The role of attributions is then explained in parent-friendly terms, and the parents are provided with exercises to help them understand the importance of attributions and how they can develop skills for working with them productively. The chapter provides guidance in helping parents deal with the often troubling issues of homework and schoolwork, including helping the child organize his homework and deal with distractions. Many children with ADHD think they are on top of things, only to be surprised when their grades come out and they discover how much of their schoolwork is missing. There is a chart in this chapter that helps the child and the parent monitor the child's schoolwork on an ongoing basis. This chapter also recommends ways for the parents to help their child develop better skills in diverse areas, such as sequencing and empathy for others, and using everyday activities, such as playing games and eating dinner to teach the child important cognitive and interpersonal skills. Coping with transitions and teaching organizational skills are also examined. Helping children with ADHD develop their internal abilities to regulate their behavior is also important. This chapter discusses ways to help the child use verbal mediation to improve his rule-governed behavior, and I examine various ways to help a child with self-soothing and with developing better control of his aggression. The problems with separation and inconsistency in parenting that arise when a parent travels are addressed here. This chapter also explores how parents' underlying feelings and beliefs about the child influence their parenting effectiveness. In addition, a simple but effective technique for putting the child in charge of his behavioral change is presented.

Chapter 8 addresses how parents can utilize each other's strengths and understand their own vulnerabilities in order to parent more effectively as a team. I explore how to guide parents to understand the situations in which they are most and least effective, and ways in which they can gracefully let their spouse take over, change their expectations of the situation to keep themselves saner, use humor, and divide responsibilities more effectively. Parents can be helped to cope with their own emotional reactions during stressful situations, put their emotions on the back burner, and use empathy to parent more effectively. Guidance is also provided for helping parents give each other feedback and assistance and listen to each other, in ways that do not exacerbate conflict. Dealing with different comfort levels with disciplinary techniques, delaying responding to children who are demanding, praising one's spouse, and getting one's child off to school in the morning are some of the other topics explored.

Chapter 9 discusses coparenting after separation or divorce. The chapter provides guidance to the clinician in helping the parents help the child keep a mental image of the noncustodial parent, cope with the different rules in the two households, and deal with transitions between the two homes. Keeping the child out of parental conflicts is also covered. This chapter helps parents understand the confusion over authority that divorced parents often unwittingly generate. Finally, the parents are helped to weigh the benefits and drawbacks of different types of custodial arrangements.

Chapter 10 discusses medication, the attitudes toward medication that parents bring to the clinician's office, and ways to help the parents sort out their beliefs from reality. Parents are helped to weigh the potential benefits and risks of medication.

Chapter 11 discusses helping parents assess the effectiveness of the help their child is receiving. With all the advice, techniques, and information that a parent has to sort through, it can be difficult to tell whether all of this is actually helping the child. Questionnaires and rating scales that might be useful at home and in school for tracking the child's improvement are presented.

Chapter 12 discusses helping parents with their self-examination of their parenting skills and how they can improve. They are helped to assess their competencies and weaknesses, to set goals for self-improvement and monitor their progress, to examine their anger (both at the child and at the spouse) and understand how irrational anger can get in the way of effective parenting, and to monitor their anger and set goals for controlling it. This chapter also emphasizes the value of parents learning from one another and setting aside times to give feedback to each other. The importance of the time parents spend with their families and getting support from the community is also addressed.

Chapter 13 discusses the question of whether one of the parents has ADHD. This chapter helps parents review their own symptoms and histories and come to terms with their own ADHD. The trials of being an adult with ADHD parenting a child with ADHD are discussed, as is the interaction of the parent's impulsivity, distractibility, and anger with the child's.

Chapter 14 guides the parents in assessing what progress they have made and where they want to go from here. It is an opportunity to take stock of the goals set and achieved, and of what the parents have learned about themselves and their spouses.

Chapter 15 discusses the clinician's working with parents on the influence that their own parents have had on their parental abilities. It looks at the possible underlying reasons parents get stuck. Treatment can break down because the parent could not or would not follow through with even simple plans, with no adequate explanation. The parenting that parents received affects not only their own behavior as parents, but also the relationship they form with their spouse. Couples get stuck in their roles and assumptions about parents, children, men, and women. It is often helpful for the parents to explore their own family-of-origin issues. The dilemmas and difficult decisions that parents of children with ADHD face when their own parents and relatives do not understand the disorder and do not support their parenting are examined. Finally, being able to get good parenting for oneself through parenting one's own child is discussed.

Chapter 16 offers some final thoughts to put this work in perspective.

I hope this book will prove useful for clinicians and parents, and that they will find it a valuable resource to work with over time. I welcome comments and feedback. Please send them to:

Edward H. Jacobs, Ph.D.
12 Parmenter Road
Londonderry, NH 03053

❖ CHAPTER 1 ❖

The Therapeutic Relationship

THE THERAPEUTIC STANCE

Practitioners of different therapeutic modalities have different perspectives on the type of therapist–patient relationship that is most beneficial. In the analytic tradition, there is the emphasis on therapeutic neutrality and the therapist becoming the repository of the patient's transferences. In the family therapy tradition, there is more of an emphasis on an active therapeutic stance, with therapists using their understanding of the family system to experiment with different interventions that are designed to reorient the alliances and communication patterns within the family. In the behavioral and cognitive-behavioral models, therapists take more of a teaching and guiding role, prescribing specific behaviors for the patient to try out, which are tailored to specific symptoms or problems. In all of these models, there has been a lively debate about the value and the risk of therapist self-disclosure, the overuse of therapist directiveness, and the practice of therapeutic passivity.

In working with parents of children with attention-deficit/hyperactivity disorder (ADHD), there seems to be an emphasis on helping the parents understand the nature of the disorder and helping them implement techniques to control the environment and manage their child's behavior. However, in the effort to convey our understanding to parents and help them to become better behavior managers, the fact that our relationship with these parents is a therapeutic one should not be lost. The value of traditional therapeutic neutrality and abstinence is that it helps the therapist maintain clear boundaries with the patient. The more involved and active the therapist is in influencing the patient's day-to-day life, the greater is the vulnerability to boundary violations. Therefore, we have to be vigilant in maintaining the therapeutic quality of our relationships with the families we serve.

In working with parents of children with ADHD therapists should not take a passive stance. However, that does not mean that there are no limits on their activity. Therapists are actively involved in imparting their knowledge of ADHD, parenting methods, and the science and technology of behavior to the parents. They are actively involved in offering suggestions and working with the parents cooperatively as part of a team. However, even with this active and involved therapeutic stance, the concepts of neutrality, abstinence, and appropriate boundaries must be kept in mind.

The parents will inevitably reveal conflicts in their system, which can take many forms. There can be a disagreement over how seriously the parents view the child's problems, or over parenting styles such as who is too strict and who is too lenient. There can be a strong disagreement between the parents over a possible medication trial, and ambivalence about the use of medication. Parents often experience internal conflicts over how strict and withholding or giving and indulging to be to their children. How many second chances should they give? When do they draw the line and take privileges away? When do they give in? When do they stand firm?

Therapists might have a clear idea of what would be best for the child in many of these cases. In their experience, they might have found that this type of child responds very well to stimulant medication, and that for the parents not to follow up with a consultation with the child's physician would be a mistake. One parent might be ready to go ahead with this, and might be appropriately fearful of another school year being wasted if the child does not have the benefits of medication. The other parent, however, might be averse to medication, and might even subscribe to some myths about medication, citing misinformation about it.

In situations like this the therapist must walk a fine line between being the knowledgeable expert and being neutral, facilitating the process of the parents resolving their own conflicts without solving them for the parents. The doubts of the skeptical parent must be respected and even valued. We cannot know for sure what will happen if the parents make certain decisions and not others.

> I had a rather humbling experience in this area. I was working with two parents on coparenting their 7-year-old ADHD son after their divorce. The mother, who found the child's behavior to be unmanageable, wanted to have a trial of medication. The child's pediatrician firmly supported this. The father was wary about medication and had amassed a great deal of negative information, including scare stories that had circulated in the media and on the Internet. Since I had evaluated and diagnosed the boy, I had seen firsthand the nature of his symptoms, which I believed were substantial. I immediately had negative feelings about what I considered to be the father's obstinacy, and told him what I knew about the benefits and risks of medication in as neutral a manner as I could. I asked the mother to hold off on her insistence that their son be prescribed medication until I was able to contact the teacher to get her assessment of how he was doing in school. From what I had seen of him, I expected this boy to need medication to function adequately in school.
>
> When I spoke to the teacher, however, I received a generally favorable report. She acknowledged that the child did behave immaturely at times and often was off-task, but that he responded to the teacher's cueing and redirection, and that his work was actually of good quality.
>
> I came to see the wisdom of holding off on the medication trial. However, now I had to respect the mother's sense of urgency about

the child's behavior at home with his sister, and her belief that he could be doing even better in school if medication could help him focus more.

I had to allow the parents to work this one out for themselves, but felt that I could help them to be more scientific in monitoring their child's behavior at their respective homes and at school, and in knowing what questions to ask themselves and the teacher in order to get a better handle on his behavior.

WHEN PARENTS CHALLENGE THE THERAPIST

A parent's doubts and questions about medication or behavior management can be presented in extreme form—as obstinacy or a direct challenge to the authority of the therapist or of the other parent. Therapists working with parents of children with ADHD must be prepared to be confronted, sometimes harshly. They must have insight into their own issues with authority in order to avoid unexpected countertransferential reactions to the parents. They must ask themselves: "How do I deal with challenges to my authority, my expertise?" "What kind of authority am I?" "What kind of authorities were my parents?" "How can I be more flexible in my reaction to challenges to my authority?"

It is wise to keep in mind that the parents of children with ADHD are often having their authority challenged in important areas of their lives—at home by their children and at school by teachers and administrators. Fathers, who often see their children's behavior in a very different light than mothers, often come into therapy expecting not to be believed, and expecting to have their authority challenged by their wives and by the therapist. Underneath the bluster that some men exhibit are feelings of vulnerability and of being an outsider. It is also difficult for many men to put themselves and their families in the hands of another person. For a lot of men, seeking professional help of any kind, but especially psychological help, diminishes the sense of control and the role of omnipotent protector that they have been socialized to assume.

Fathers who question many of the therapist's recommendations should not be dismissed out of hand as unreasonable saboteurs of therapy. Rather, the therapist should give these men the message that their doubts and questions are welcomed. This is at times surprising for the father when the control struggle that he might have been expecting, or even aiming for, is removed from the table. I find that this stance by the therapist is usually welcomed by the father, and that the therapist ends up with an ally in the family.

There is nothing to be afraid of in examining any parent's doubts. Out of concern for the child, parents will want to make sure that they are doing the right thing. Accepting things at face value might not indicate the most careful or thoughtful parent. So a father's doubts and questioning should be understood as his care and concern for doing what is best for his child, and his insistence on taking responsibility for his child's care rather than blindly trusting others.

It is important to communicate to the parents from the first that they are the bosses of their family. The way to deal with challenges and obstinacy, in general, is to give them credence. The exception to this is when they become a form of acting out. It is a well-known analytic principle that acting out has to be contained before any further therapeutic work is possible. The behavior has to be confronted directly and firmly, but kindly.

> After prolonged negotiations with one couple who could not agree on any way to compromise, and after several suggestions and compromises had been proposed by the wife and rejected by the husband, the husband still insisted that they do things his way, which repeatedly had been ineffective. His belief was that he was right, and if his wife would just agree and go along with him, there would be no problem. He was apparently blind to the shortcomings of his way.
>
> Finally, I addressed the husband directly: "Mr. Smith, for years you have tried to do things your way and you have failed. Trying it your way has landed you in a psychologist's office. We can either continue to try it your way, which by all the evidence that we have will lead to failure, or we can try it my way. It's your choice."

I try to appeal to the scientist in the parents. I take this position: let's look at what has not worked and stop repeating our mistakes, and let's look at what has worked, even briefly, and build on what that teaches us. When I present the parents with the evidence, they usually make the sensible choice.

THERAPIST'S SELF-DISCLOSURE

Another challenge to therapeutic boundaries is the matter of therapeutic self-disclosure. Parents who are facing the daunting challenges involved in raising a child with ADHD often report feelings of failure and inadequacy. They often feel that they are abnormal. They try approaches that every other parent tries, but these approaches never work for them like they work for other parents. Their good parental intuition tells them to do one thing, but that often backfires, leaving them in a state of befuddlement. Even normal parent–child problems contribute to the parents' sense of inadequacy. They might react to typical control struggles with the belief that these things don't happen in normal families with adequate parents.

In these situations, it is tempting to try to give the parents the message that much of what they are experiencing are the typical stresses and strains of child rearing, and nothing that signifies their own inadequacies. The depression and self-doubt experienced by many parents of children with ADHD can be debilitating and can induce a sense of helplessness that makes them even more ineffective and less able to try new things. If we can normalize them in their own minds, we might counteract these depressive and helpless thoughts.

It therefore might be therapeutically useful for therapists to share a personal anecdote to illustrate that they have experienced something similar in the normal course of parenting children. If this relieves some of the helplessness and reverses the psychological immobility of the parents, it can free them up to try new things and work together more effectively.

One father was frustrated at the rejection he experienced whenever he came home from work. His daughter wouldn't talk to him or play with him. He was already feeling inadequate because of his daughter's behavior problems, and this rejection made him so angry that he often yelled at her and argued with his wife. I decided to share with the couple my experience coming home from work, being excited to see my own daughter, and having her tell me that she did not want me to talk to her or ask her questions about her day. I explained to them how some young children have difficulty handling transitions, and that a parent coming home at the end of the day imposed a radical change in the environment with which the child had to cope. Furthermore, being asked questions by the returning parent was putting even greater demands on the child, and certain children could be expected to react with resistance. This was the child's attempt either to wish away the challenge that the environment was imposing on her, or to titrate some of the stimulation which seemed so overwhelming, or to adapt to a little bit at a time. Some children needed more time than others to adapt to this disruption in their environment.

Hearing that the therapist, whom the father considered to be a competent parent (this is a case where positive transference need not be questioned), had experienced some of the same rejection from his own child enabled the father to feel some relief and to put this occurrence into perspective, rather than treating it as one more piece of evidence of his inadequacy. We could then discuss ways to help him to keep from engaging in control struggles with his daughter and even use humor to detoxify the situation.

Although parent guidance work might be one of the few therapeutic endeavors in which self-disclosure might be appropriate some of the time, the choice to self-disclose must be undertaken with great caution. Because of the possible dangers of self-disclosure, I would err on the side of nondisclosure if there is reason to feel uncomfortable about it. Keep in mind that, no matter how useful the therapist might think self-disclosure is, clients have come to talk about and hear about their own child, not the therapist's. What the therapist might regard as a nice illustration from his personal life, and an effective joining with the client, they might regard as an unwanted intrusion on the professional time for which they are paying.

Therapists have to consider, in every case, if they are self-disclosing because of their own needs or because of the client's needs. Therapists have to check their needs to talk too much, especially about themselves. Parenting stress is a topic that especially pulls for empathy, sharing of experiences, and a need to be seen as competent. Therapists will feel a pull to share their own experiences, which will derive as much from their own needs as it will from their desire to help their patients. Contributing to therapists' desire to self-disclose may be their need (of which they might be unaware) to be seen as competent, to be seen as "regular people," to be admired or to be liked by the patient.

It is also tempting to assume that what therapists consider to be similarities in their and their client's experience are seen the same way by the client. But the client might consider a therapist's experiences irrelevant to his and might not say so, out of politeness. Therapists talking about themselves might therefore engender some unspoken resentment in the client. Even if the therapists' experiences are relevant, the client might not believe that they could truly experience the same degree of difficulty or incompetence that he experiences, because of their elevated status. Furthermore, some clients do not want to believe that the therapist could be as incompetent as they are, or that the therapist's family could have the same difficulties as theirs does because of their need to maintain the therapist's elevated status in their minds. Such are the vagaries of transference, a phenomenon whose importance has been long recognized by the analytic community and, unfortunately, given short shrift by behavioral and cognitive-behavioral writers.

Since the transferential expectations of each client will differ, therapists must tread very delicately in the areas of self-disclosure, and must try to understand how the client sees them, not just how they want to appear to the client. This does not mean that therapists should not take risks. They cannot do productive therapy without risk. However, the risks must be thought out and the reasons to take them must be clear. Therapists must also be attuned to the consequences of the risks that they take—how the client reacts and whether the reaction is productive. The therapeutic relationship deserves as much attention in this type of work as it does in psychoanalytic work.

THERAPISTS WEAR MANY HATS

Therapists working with parents of children with ADHD wear many hats. They are first and foremost engaged to help the parents resolve difficulties, employing their special expertise as mental health professionals. Within this role, therapists can do several things. They can guide the parents in working out their own conflicts in their own ways by understanding each parent's point of view and by helping them to integrate their different perspectives. Therapists can also make suggestions, give advice, and encourage the parents to be scientific in assessing whether these suggestions actually work for them. Rather than imposing the advice on the parents as "experts," therapists can use their expertise to make suggestions and point the way to a possible course of action.

Therapists must always respect the fact that those methods that the parents try are attempted in their homes while they are living their lives. Therapists do not have to live with their own advice. If something is not working for the parents, the therapist cannot assume that the parents are failing or resisting. It is up to the therapist to understand the client and investigate why something that might seem sensible to the therapist is not working and to come up with a better approach.

Parents already come in feeling like failures. Consulting a therapist might be experienced as a narcissistic blow to many of them, even if they are eager to get help and look forward to the consultation. It is important to respect the parents' feelings of inadequacy and accept them as the norm. It is also important to find out what the parents have done that has worked. Many parents will describe their attempts at behavior management as failures. However, upon close scrutiny, it becomes apparent that many of their abandoned plans worked for a week or two before getting "old." What the parents perceive as failures can actually be seen as short-lived successes.

Anything that has worked for a week or two has worked. It is typically found that the ADHD child thrives on novelty. Things get old rather quickly. If a behavior plan worked for a week or two, it was probably based on sound behavior management principles and stopped working because the parents did not know to build in some novelty, to change it somewhat, in order to keep it engaging and stimulating enough for the child. These plans should not be seen as static entities but must evolve as the interests of the ADHD child change over time.

The corollary to the behavior plan that works for a week or two and then stops working is the plan that works well, improves the child's behavior, and then is not followed because the child's behavior is better, resulting in the behavior eventually deteriorating. Many parents abandon behavior plans after they have worked so well that the parents think that they no longer need them. Parents would be more accurate in thinking, "The behavior is better *because* we have the behavior plan."

Many parents need help in appreciating that ADHD is a disorder that does not simply go away, and that it requires constant work and effort. This type of motivation often needs the support of the therapist for two exhausted and overwhelmed parents to maintain. When things start to improve, when a behavior plan is effective and the parents do well with it, it is a natural inclination for the parents to let down their guard, breathe a sigh of relief, and think: "Problem solved. Let's move on." The parents need the therapist's, and each other's, support to maintain the vigilance that this work requires.

LENGTH OF TREATMENT

Another concern that therapists have is the length of treatment. We are faced with a reimbursement environment that values and pays for short-term skill building. This might be all that certain parents need.

However, we must keep in mind that ADHD is a lifelong disorder and therefore a lifelong challenge for the children and parents affected by it. It is a chronic condition. Health professionals recognize that chronic medical conditions, such as diabetes and heart disease, require a lifetime of management. Like these other conditions, the symptoms of ADHD change over time. The management skills of the patient and family need to change over time as well and, since ADHD is a developmental disorder beginning in childhood and lasting into adulthood, the interaction between the disorder and the individual's developmental level changes over time as well.

Skill development for the patient and the parents, therefore, is hardly a static thing. There are some families who will work with a therapist for a brief period of time, leave, and never consult again. There are probably far more with whom the therapist will have a relationship over a long span of time, either by working with them first regularly and then more intermittently for years, or by working with them for several brief spans of time that are separated by years. Some parents will leave with a set of skills for helping one child, only to call years later for help for a younger sibling who is exhibiting symptoms.

Although there is standard information that we communicate to patients and parents about the disorder, and techniques that we typically teach them, each family's need for intervention will be unique to that family, and there is no way to standardize that aspect of care. Each patient's and family's need for frequency and intensity of services must be negotiated on a case-by-case basis.

One example of a short-term intervention involved 6-year-old Matthew, who was in the second grade. He was a bright boy, but he could not sit still or focus for more than a few minutes. He did all right in kindergarten, but the demands of first grade were just too much for him. His parents never suspected that he might have ADHD because he was so bright and did relatively well in spite of his difficulties.

Once Matthew was diagnosed, he was prescribed stimulant medication, and his teacher responded by making more eye contact, engaging him more frequently, and breaking down his work into small chunks while providing him with frequent breaks and feedback.

Matthew's parents developed effective behavior management skills. Because they were able to form a good working alliance with Matthew's school, and because their skills and the medication continued to prove effective in managing Matthew's behavior, the brief diagnostic and clinical contact was enough to help them get Matthew through elementary school. The parents' working with Matthew's doctor and his teachers regularly was sufficient to keep him and his parents on track.

An example of a long-term relationship is Mark, whom I first saw in middle school and continued seeing until the end of high school with variable frequency. In middle school, Mark was very immature socially and was teased a lot by his peers. This teasing often resulted in Mark's seeking revenge and provoking physical fights with his adversaries, in spite of the fact that he was smaller and weaker than most of them. Mark also delighted in criticizing and making fun of non-teaching employees at the school, such as maintenance workers and secretaries, whom he thought he could look down on.

At that stage, Mark's parents' concerns were mainly about his social and interpersonal difficulties, not his academics. Mark was intelligent and his grades were fairly good, although inconsistent. Intervention helped him to stop behaving in provocative ways to peers and adults, and to follow the rules and behavioral expectations of his school.

As Mark got older, his social skills improved, his provocative behavior decreased, and he made many friends. In the upper grades of middle school, his parents became concerned about the amount of time he was spending on-line chatting with friends and strangers. Mark seemed to lose track of time when he was on his computer, and he was unaware of how much his computer time interfered with getting his homework done. Furthermore, Mark was unprepared for the increased work load and organizational demands of the upper grades in middle school. He had more long-term assignments to keep track of, more books to read, and more activities to juggle. He was frequently late handing in assignments, and he often did his homework and then failed to hand it in at all because he did not know where he had put it.

At this stage, Mark needed help developing a better understanding of the passage of time and better skills at managing his time. He needed to appreciate that his time on the computer was taking time away from completing his work, and that this was affecting his grades in the long run. He needed to develop a better system of placing his completed homework in the same place every day and monitoring whether he handed it in when he got to class.

Later, in high school, Mark's grades began to suffer seriously. Although he was certain that he studied for tests and completed his work, his progress reports always reflected some low test grades and incomplete assignments. Mark was doing a poor job of monitoring his home behavior on a day-to-day basis. Furthermore, he had developed a friendship with a girl who his parents thought was manipulative and destructive to Mark. All of these issues brought Mark into more frequent and severe conflicts with his parents than he had experienced previously. He became more concerned about his privacy and shut his parents out, which of course made them more worried and caused them to probe more into his life.

Family therapy helped to lessen some of the tension at home and establish some ground rules for privacy and responsibility, on the condition that if Mark did not live up to his responsibilities, as he said he could, he would have to sacrifice some of his privacy by having his parents take over more of the monitoring of his behavior and set stricter limits on his time. We also developed ways for Mark to monitor his own work completion and academic progress. He agreed to follow through with these efforts by working with his school counselor.

Mark also used our counseling to examine the problems that his relationship with his girlfriend caused him, and as a result became more assertive and better able to set limits in the relationship. Issues of being taken advantage of in his friendships were explored later in counseling.

There were periods when I was meeting with Mark every week, periods when I was meeting with him biweekly or monthly, and periods when I did not meet with him at all and did not know if I would see him again.

CORRECTIVE EMOTIONAL EXPERIENCE

The relationship that parents have with their child's therapist also takes on characteristics of a *corrective emotional experience*. Although this term is common in psychodynamic circles, we must appreciate that, while our focus might be on skill building, the parents' skill development takes place in the context of a therapeutic relationship.

We are more than just coaches or teachers or consultants to parents. It is often with us that, for the first time, the parents don't feel like "freaks" as parents. Many of them have felt outside of the mainstream for so long. Their children don't behave the way other children do; their friends look down on their parenting skills; they hear their friends boast about their children's accomplishments, which seem to be beyond the reach of their own children; and what works for other parents does not work for them. Most of these parents are just as loving and skilled as any others, but they feel like failures. The understanding and acceptance offered by the therapist helps these parents to experience themselves in a new, positive light, as well as to see their spouses in a positive light as well. The therapist, in some ways, parents the parents, giving them what they need emotionally so they are freed up to parent their children in more effective ways.

HELPING PARENTS TO BE ADVOCATES

Another role for therapists that might be different from their role in other types of therapy is encouraging the parents to become advocates for the child, which sometimes involves helping them to take bold steps that they have not taken previously. Parents often feel more confident in understanding and dealing with their child's behavior at home after meeting with a therapist. However, there still remains great concern about how the child will do in school and in community activities, such as sports, scouts, and clubs. They have often tried to deal with the outside world peaceably, so as not to make waves and to have everything go smoothly for their child. However, for many, this approach has not worked, and they find themselves increasingly dissatisfied with the lack of understanding or help offered by the child's school or by community organizations. The therapist often takes on the role of encouraging parents to assertively and persistently advocate for the child's needs with the school and other organizations. The parents might need encouragement to "ruffle some feathers" or challenge some rules.

HELPING PARENTS TO BE MORE EFFECTIVE

The therapist is also useful in helping the parents to become more objective observers of their child and themselves. Although the therapist does express interest in the parents' feelings and biases, the bottom line is always what works and what doesn't work. Parents might hold on to a dearly held belief about parenting, such as disobedient children need to be spanked, or punishments that last for weeks at a time are more effective than brief punishments. The therapist will help them focus on whether or not the practices they are using are effective. Rather than arguing the point with the parent or mediating a disagreement between two parents, the therapist can ask the parents how each approach is working. The chances are good that many of these beliefs are not working, or the child would not be in therapy.

In contrast, some parents come in thinking that nothing they have done has worked. By looking at the results of their actions more objectively, they can often see that many of their efforts have worked, only not for as long a time or as completely as they expected or would have liked. The parents' expectation often is that something must work completely and forever in order to be deemed effective. Such expectations are unrealistic, and set them up to think of themselves as failures and to feel bad. What is more realistic is to expect solutions to work for short periods of time, and to expect that any solution, no matter how good, will not be effective in all circumstances.

WHAT IS THE PREFERRED THERAPEUTIC MODALITY?

Parents often ask: "How does this work? Do you see us or our child? Should the child come to the first appointment?" I usually ask the parents to bring the child to the first interview. I tell the parents that if there are things they are uncomfortable discussing in front of their child and would be more comfortable discussing in private, they should introduce me to the child at a later time. Usually, the child knows there is a problem because by the time parents get to the point of calling me, they have made it painfully clear to the child that they are troubled by his behavior. The child has probably been in on countless discussions about how the parents can help him or how his behavior is causing difficulty for himself or the family.

I count on my skills to keep the meeting from getting out of hand and turning into a "blame the child" session. Usually, the parents respond to my air of collaboration and concern and to my positive demeanor toward the child, even if the child is negativistic toward me. If the meeting does take a turn for the worse, I either redirect the parents or excuse the child for a while and speak to the parents alone.

I like to see how the child responds and reacts to his parents' description of their concerns about him and the family. I get to observe if the child is polite and respectful, if he is defiant, contrary and oppositional, if he cuts the parents off when they try to speak, if he crosses his arms over his chest and refuses to speak, if he fidgets in his chair, if his affect is appropriate or not, if he externalizes blame, if he distorts reality, and if he listens to the parents and to me. I get a sense of how verbal and intelligent the child is.

I also get a sense if there is a problem with a sibling from the child's perspective, something that might have been discounted by the parents. I get to see if the child thinks that his sibling is favored, if he is physically attacked by the sibling, if his own attacks on the sibling are provoked in any way, and if the parents respond differently to his transgressions than they do to the sibling's. I hear if the child understands the parents' commands and disciplinary methods in the same way that the parents intend them.

I get to see how well the parents listen to the child, if they discount his perspective, if they blame him for everything, if one parent sees things differently from the other, whether these differences are acted out in how the parents discipline the child, if they indulge the child by listening to him too much instead of taking action when they should, if they relate to the child out of guilt or anger, if they are afraid of and controlled by their child's anger, if they cut each other off when addressing the child, and if the child listens to and obeys each parent differently.

At the initial meeting, I get some clarification as to what I am being hired to do. The first issue to decide is whether I am going to assess the child for ADHD in order to make or clarify the diagnosis. If the child has already been assessed and diagnosed to the parents' satisfaction, then my role will be one of therapist or counselor.

After getting a sense from the parents as to what they need and want, I can further define how I am going to work with them. My role can take a number of forms. If I am going to be counseling the family and child, I have to ask myself several questions about their needs, such as:

Is the child's behavior hard to control at home and/or at school?

Does the child have difficulty regulating his emotional state?

Are the parents working together effectively as a team?

Do the parents need to learn different parenting skills?

How well do the parents understand the nature of ADHD and how well do they accept that their child has a biologically based condition?

Do the parents feel confident that their child is getting what he needs in school?

Do the parents have adequate supports themselves?

Asking myself these questions helps me to determine how best to intervene. Usually after meeting with the parents and the child (which sometimes also includes the siblings), I set up a time to meet with the child alone to get a sense of the child apart from the parents. Depending on the age of the child, I might talk to him about his likes and dislikes; his home and school life; what he would like to change about his family, his school, or himself; and how he handles situations that make him angry or frustrated. I try to get a sense of what he would like to be able to do differently.

I also get a sense of the child's developmental level by assessing whether his interests are age-appropriate and whether his social skills and problem-solving skills are mature or immature. I often ask the child to do a human figure drawing and a kinetic family drawing as both a quick measure of his visual-motor integration and as a projective technique. I sometimes invite the child to select a toy or a game to play with and assess his vulnerability to regression (does he select toys typical of a much younger age, or does he express immature themes in his play?), his ability to include another person in his play, his ability to differentiate fantasy from reality, and his willingness to take turns and follow rules and thereby demonstrate the ability to delay gratification and accept the constraints that reality places on our need for wish-fulfillment.

The child will show me how well he separates from his parents, whether he is too willing to trust a stranger, and how well he copes with the expectation that he will clean up after himself and leave at the appointed time. By listening to the child, I will get a sense of how he communicates verbally. It is often difficult to get a real sense of this with his parents in the room because they often answer for the child or "translate" for me what they hear him saying. If the child has articulation or expressive language problems, the parents will be more attuned to interpreting the child's speech, and their ability to interact with the child productively might make him more understandable than would otherwise be the case. Therefore, meeting with the child individually gives me a clearer sense as to whether there are any speech problems that might get in the way of the child's communicating with the outside world. I get to hear any articulation problems and get to experience any cumulative confusion that comes from not having his words frequently clarified by his parents. I get to hear what the child's spontaneous speech is like. Does he initiate verbal interactions? Does he comment on toys? Does he spontaneously communicate pleasure, surprise, or distress? Does he ask for things? Does he act instead of speak? Does he assert his needs? I also get to hear how the child uses syntax. Does he order words correctly? Does he use full sentences? Are the subjects and objects of his sentences and questions clear?

Seeing how the child responds to my request to draw pictures gives me a sense of how the child responds to directions to do something that he might not want to do as much as he would like to do other things. I get a sense of how the child resists when he doesn't want to do something, and how he can negotiate a compromise so that he complies with expectations but still gets his needs respected. I get a sense of how important it is for the child to be in control of an adult or an unfamiliar situation.

Having the child draw also gives me clues to self-esteem issues. Many children are eager to draw and like to show off what they have produced. Other children make many self-deprecating comments throughout the drawing tasks. If a child chooses to show her drawings to her parents, I get to observe how the parents respond to this. Do they praise the child? Do they use an excited and interested tone of voice? Do they comment on "errors" the child might have made? Do they remark that someone or something in the picture does not look like the person or thing it was intended to represent? I therefore get a sense of the parent–child interaction around the child's productions. Although my office is a controlled, structured setting, the child gives me some information about her ability to regulate her internal state, whether that has to do with her emotions or behavior.

After meeting with the parents and the child, and the child alone, I give feedback to the parents about how I might be of help to them. Parents are sometimes surprised that I am not going to be meeting with their child exclusively and "fixing" her. These parents need to be told that they might be the best teachers for their child and that I can help them develop the necessary skills. In this role, I can help them develop more effective and consistent management techniques that they can use together. I can train them to intervene with their child more effectively, communicate and coordinate with each other better, and teach their child to calm down and better regulate herself.

Sometimes it makes sense to include meetings with the child alone. These meetings are useful if I am going to teach the child relaxation or self-soothing techniques, or if I am going to help the child directly to develop better social skills, such as turn taking. I might also ask the child to collaborate with me at decreasing the number of arguments she is involved in at home, making that a project between the two of us instead of involving the parents. I might fill the parents in on what we are doing so they can support it. I explain this technique later in this book.

The parents might be at a loss as to how to work with the school and how to become better advocates for their child. They might need advice or coaching on setting up a meeting with the appropriate personnel, requesting an evaluation, or getting feedback on how their child is doing. They might need help in asserting themselves with a system in relation to which they feel unskilled and helpless. Some parents might want me to take an active role in the school, either by observing their child in classes, attending meetings with the school team, or conferring with the teachers or the principal on the telephone.

There are other times when the family system as a whole is in so much conflict and turmoil that family therapy sessions need to be scheduled. These are not just for the purpose of teaching parenting techniques or teaching the child self-control. They are for actively working on complex family interactions and alliances, to develop better boundaries between the generations and between individuals in the system, or to promote greater cohesiveness among family members who have become more distant over time.

I don't automatically assume that I will take on any of these roles until I assess the situation and judge where I can be of most help to the child and the parents.

❖ CHAPTER 2 ❖

What Is ADHD?: Explaining It to Parents

When I undertake to explain ADHD to parents, I try to give them some basic understanding of the disorder without oversimplifying it or complicating it with too much technical detail. It is also important to anticipate and address common areas of misinformation or confusion

The terms *ADHD* and *attention-deficit disorder (ADD)* are often used interchangeably. ADHD is the formal diagnostic classification that is used by the American Psychiatric Association (1994). The diagnosis of ADHD includes three subtypes. The first includes those individuals who primarily have problems with paying attention. These people are not hyperactive, nor do they display prominent symptoms of impulsivity. They are therefore identified with the subtype of ADHD called *Predominantly Inattentive Type*. The second subtype includes those individuals whose symptoms primarily consist of hyperactivity and/or impulsivity, and are identified with the subtype *Predominantly Hyperactive-Impulsive Type*. Those individuals who exhibit clinically significant signs of both inattention and hyperactivity-impulsivity, are designated with the third subtype, *Combined Type*.

The term *ADD* is not a formal diagnosis. It is commonly used as a shorthand way of referring to the disorder, or to indicate someone with ADHD, *Predominantly Inattentive Type*.

ADHD is a neurologically based disorder that affects the regulation of attention and behavior. There are symptoms and characteristics that are commonly identified with ADHD, although it is important to keep in mind that every child with ADHD is unique and has his own combination of characteristics. Not every child with ADHD has every symptom, and no one symptom occurs in every child with ADHD. Furthermore, the symptoms vary in their intensity, in the settings in which they occur, in how consistently or inconsistently they occur, and in the degree to which they interfere with the child's functioning.

ADHD occurs in boys and girls, although research has found that it tends to occur with greater frequency in boys. How much more prevalent it is in boys is a matter of debate. However, there are many girls with ADHD, many of whom are inattentive and not hyperactive and therefore get overlooked.

The three symptoms that are agreed upon by professionals to be the defining characteristics of ADHD are (1) inattention, (2) impulsivity, and (3) hyperactivity. The ADHD child exhibits these characteristics much more frequently and severely than his peers typically do, and these symptoms interfere with his functioning in important areas of his life, such as home, school, peer activities, and recreational pursuits. These characteristics, therefore, have to be developmentally inappropriate. That is, they have to be atypical for the child's age. To warrant a diagnosis, they also have to appear in a developmentally inappropriate form before the age of 7, and have to last at least six months.

Inattention is a multifaceted concept. Some ADHD children are described as being "distractible." This means that when they are trying to perform one task, their attention is easily diverted by things that other children would be able to screen out, such as background noises, people talking, or a car passing outside the window. They can even be distracted by thoughts and feelings they are having that are irrelevant to the task at hand. These children have difficulty with *fo-*

cused attention. Some children can focus their attention well on one thing at a time but they cannot maintain this focus for long. These children have what is commonly called a short attention span, or poor *sustained attention.*

Other children have problems with *attentional shift.* They focus very well on tasks that are highly interesting to them, but their parents and teachers get very frustrated when they try to get them to change their activities. They can get stuck on something and have great difficulty leaving it to go on to something else when they are required to do so.

Another aspect of attention is the *orienting response* that tells us there is something in the environment to pay attention to. Many children with ADHD, for example, have to be told to listen (to orient themselves) before being spoken to.

Selective attention describes the ability to tune in to the relevant stimuli or information from the environment and screen out what is not important. It is the ability to select from the multitude of stimuli in the environment those cues that inform us about what will be rewarded or punished.

Children's attention might vary according to the sensory modality that they are using at the time. Some children have more difficulty attending to auditory information and others have more difficulty with visual information. Therefore, an attention deficit might be noticeable when one sensory modality is required to succeed on a task, and not when the other modality is employed.

It is important to understand that children with ADHD can and do exhibit good attention much of the time. This is particularly true on tasks that are highly interesting or rewarding to them, and that have a high degree of stimulation and use a lot of novelty. It is not totally accurate, therefore, to say that these children have a *deficit* in attention. It might be more accurate to say that they have an *inconsistency* in their attention, or a problem regulating it.

Impulsivity refers to the tendency to act without thinking, to fail to inhibit one's actions when it is socially appropriate to do so, and to blurt things out, to the displeasure of peers and adults. It makes these children accident prone, and prone to rejection by peers and punishment by adults.

Hyperactivity refers to excessive motor activity that is inappropriate for one's age. Hyperactive children are always on the go. Some are not so obviously active, with a lot of gross motor movement, but are more fidgety and restless. They have a hard time sitting still without moving or squirming. It is not unusual for older children with ADHD to appear to be sitting still, but to feel restless internally and have their minds wandering while their bodies are staying seated.

ADHD children who are predominantly hyperactive or impulsive tend to get noticed more easily and tend to receive more negative feedback than other children. Many of these children also have a problem controlling their aggression.

The children who are predominantly inattentive are often quiet and might spend a lot of time daydreaming. They are also more likely to exhibit some mild symptoms of anxiety or depression.

The American Psychiatric Association has published a set of criteria used to diagnose ADHD. The following is a list of behavioral symptoms that occur with greater frequency in the ADHD child than they do in the child without ADHD. These behaviors are considered to be examples of the inattention, impulsivity, or hyperactivity mentioned above.

Diagnostic criteria for Attention-Deficit/Hyperactivity Disorder

A. Either (1) or (2);

(1) six (or more) of the following symptoms of *inattention* have persisted for at least six months to a degree that is maladaptive and inconsistent with development level:

Inattention

(a) often fails to give close attention to details or makes careless mistakes in schoolwork, work, or other activities

(b) often has difficulty sustaining attention in tasks or play activities

(c) often does not seem to listen when spoken to directly
(d) often does not follow through on instructions and fails to finish schoolwork, chores, or duties in the workplace (not due to oppositional behavior or failure to understand instructions)
(e) often has difficulty organizing tasks and activities
(f) often avoids, dislikes, or is reluctant to engage in tasks that require sustained mental effort (such as schoolwork or homework)
(g) often loses things necessary for tasks or activities (e.g., toys, school assignments, pencils, books, or tools)
(h) is often easily distracted by extraneous stimuli
(i) is often forgetful in daily activities

(2) six (or more) of the following symptoms of *hyperactivity-impulsivity* have persisted for at least six months to a degree that is maladaptive and inconsistent with developmental level:

Hyperactivity
(a) often fidgets with hands or feet or squirms in seat
(b) often leaves seat in classroom or in other situations in which remaining seated is expected
(c) often runs about or climbs excessively in situations in which it is inappropriate (in adolescents or adults, may be limited to subjective feelings of restlessness)
(d) often has difficulty playing or engaging in leisure activities quietly
(e) is often "on the go" or often acts as if "driven by a motor"
(f) often talks excessively

Impulsivity
(g) often blurts out answers before questions have been completed
(h) often has difficulty awaiting turn

(i) often interrupts or intrudes on others (e.g., butts into conversations or games)

B. Some hyperactive-impulsive or inattentive symptoms that caused impairment were present before age 7 years.

C. Some impairment from the symptoms is present in two or more settings (e.g., at school [or work] and at home).

D. There must be clear evidence of clinically significant impairment in social, academic, or occupational functioning.

(Reprinted with permission from the *Diagnostic and Statistical Manual of Mental Disorders,* 4th edition, Copyright 1994, American Psychiatric Association).

There are other signs and symptoms, some of which are commonly considered defining characteristics of ADHD, or primary problems, and others that are considered closely associated with the core symptoms of the disorder, or secondary problems.

The problems that are considered to be an integral part of ADHD are the following:

Deficits in rule-governed behavior: This refers to difficulty conforming one's behavior to the rules in many settings, difficulty behaving in ways that will be rewarded, and difficulty avoiding behaving in ways that will be punished, within the context of a particular setting.

Deficits in reinforcement sensitivity: This indicates that the rewards and punishments that most people attend to and respond to have a weaker influence on the behavior of the ADHD child. Rewards and consequences have to be stronger, more immediate, more specific, and more varied for ADHD children.

Deficits in executive functions: ADHD children have difficulty sustaining effort over a period of time, formulating plans, developing strategies to solve problems, persisting in effort, inhibiting desires that compete with task completion, controlling alertness, organizing time and the environment, practicing solutions, considering alternatives, and remembering important information.

Deficits in anticipating the future: There is a difficulty delaying responding, analyzing a situation, mentally breaking down and reconstructing events, and using language to see things in a different way.

Secondary, but closely related, problems include the following:

Social and communication deficits: Children with ADHD typically have difficulty regulating the intensity of their interactions. They can be insensitive to social subtleties and have difficulty shifting gears, being responsive to their peers, and attending to the feelings of others or being sensitive to their treatment of others. Frequently perceived negatively by peers, they are often rejected or scapegoated.

Memory deficits: There is often a problem remembering rules and directions and a difficulty with short-term memory tasks, such as copying from the board or remembering what was studied for a test.

Response speed deficits: Children with ADHD often have difficulty performing under timed conditions, as they fail to complete their work in the time allotted.

Self-esteem deficits: Children with ADHD are typically plagued by feelings of inadequacy with their peers, in school, and with their parents. They feel like failures in meeting the expectations of others and of themselves. They often experience others as being disappointed in them, and are frequently told that they are lazy or that they don't care. This leaves many of them feeling that they are "dumb."

Problems with emotional regulation: Many parents describe their children with ADHD as being easily triggered to exhibit severe signs of anger, anxiety, or depression, provoked by events that would not trouble the ordinary person to such an extent. This is true for both the intensity of their emotional reactions and their duration. The emotional reactions of many ADHD children seem like turning on a light switch: the child is flooded with emotion that seems to be either on or off, with no in-between. Rather than experiencing gradations of emotions, such as annoyance, irritation, anger, and then rage, the child seems to go from calm to rageful without anything in between. And once such an emotional reaction starts, it can be very difficult to turn off. Whether this emotionality is one aspect of the ADHD child's characteristic impulsivity or whether it is a symptom of a related affective disorder can be difficult to sort out, but it is, nevertheless, a characteristic of many children with ADHD.

Oppositional and defiant behavior: Many ADHD children develop a pattern of avoidance of the demands and expectations that are placed on them, especially by adults. This might be a survival mechanism, used to escape from the embarrassment of not being able to perform the way others expect them to. Unfortunately, this often escalates into an attempt to control authority as well as into a conditioned pattern of negative attention-seeking.

❖ CHAPTER 3 ❖

Could My Child Have ADHD?

A parent might ask: If there is a list of symptoms, why is ADHD so hard to diagnose? I give them several reasons. First, all ADHD children are different. For example, one child might be inattentive in that she "spaces out" in class and takes four hours each night to do homework that takes most of her classmates a half hour. However, she can engage in lengthy fantasy play with dolls and puppets for hours at a time with her friends. In contrast, another child might be a bit fidgety, but eagerly participates in class and, although he rushes his work, he gets it done. When he is at home, however, he cannot sit still. He will become intensely absorbed in a television program, but only for a few minutes, and then he gets up off the couch frequently, or looks for other things to play with. Both of these children could be described as "inattentive," but each of them exhibits inattention in different ways, in different situations, and with different people.

A second reason that ADHD is difficult to diagnose is that the behaviors that are listed as symptoms are behaviors that all children exhibit to some degree and that many children without ADHD exhibit often. In fact, some parents refer to a symptom, such as "often does not seem to listen when spoken to directly," and ask, "Isn't this true for all children?" And they are correct.

What makes a symptom a symptom and not a normal behavior is that, as the diagnostic manual says, it has "persisted for at least six months" and it occurs "to a degree that is maladaptive and inconsistent with developmental level." In addition, these symptoms have to result in difficulty functioning in two or more settings. Let's look at these important considerations.

To say that a symptom has to be inconsistent with the child's developmental level is to say, for example, that although all 6-year-olds have some trouble sitting still, following directions, and dong schoolwork, the 6-year-old with ADHD has significantly greater difficulty sitting still, following directions, and getting work done than does the typical 6-year-old. The child's symptoms have to be compared with the behaviors of same age peers.

Furthermore, it is not sufficient to have these symptoms to a greater extent than other children the same age. The symptoms have to cause a problem in functioning. For example, a teacher might observe that a 7-year-old boy often fidgets with hands or feet or squirms in his seat, but that he does his work, his work seems to match his ability, and he does not disturb others around him. His grades are good and he has friends. So, although this boy might be much more fidgety than others his age, his fidgeting does not get in the way of his school performance or peer relationships.

A third consideration is that, in addition to a significant number of symptoms occurring more often than in peers and interfering with functioning, they also have to impair functioning, to some extent, in two or more settings. So, a 10-year-old might have significant difficulty waiting his turn in games, and be overly active, on the go, running excessively, and showing other signs of impulsivity and hyperactivity in peer situations, but fit in well at school and at home.

Fourth, there have to be some signs of the disorder from an early age. ADHD does not suddenly materialize in middle childhood or adolescence unless there has been some accident or medical condition that alters brain functioning. Signs and symptoms usually occur in the preschool years. However, it is common that problems in functioning are not noticed until the child enters school. There are several reasons for this. For one, children with mild symptoms, or children who are inattentive but not hyperactive, often function reasonably well in a home setting, where there is less structure and less of a demand for performance than there is in a school setting. Their behavior is often not regarded as a problem, or it is seen as a variation of normal. I have evaluated children in middle school and high school and have identified them for the first time as having ADHD. Most of these adolescents were primarily inattentive and not hyperactive, and many of them were highly intelligent. They managed to get through school, struggling much of the time, but not doing poorly enough to be identified by their schools as having significant difficulty until adolescence. Although these children's problems might not have been glaringly obvious until adolescence, when their parents looked back on their history of school performance, there were signs of ADHD all along the way that were not put into the context of a long-term problem.

Problems with early identification also arise because, although some children might be recognized as requiring more attention compared with other children (particularly by the mother), the other parent (often the father) might have a higher tolerance for such behavior ("boys will be boys," or "he's just like I was when I was a child"). Fathers might not see the worst of their children's behavior if they are not home as much as the mothers. Children usually behave worse with the parent who spends the most time with them.

A fifth consideration is that the symptoms are not better explained by another mental disorder. ADHD is largely a diagnosis made by elimination. Inattention, hyperactivity, and impulsivity are common in several other psychiatric conditions, and these conditions have to be considered and eliminated as possible causes of the symptoms before a diagnosis of ADHD can be made.

For example, a 17-year-old boy was referred to me for evaluation by his psychiatrist, who suspected that he had ADHD because of a long history of school failure, and aggressive, impulsive, and extremely socially inappropriate behavior. Although this young man met the diagnostic criteria for ADHD, his behavior, his history, and psychological testing suggested bipolar (manic depressive) disorder instead.

This diagnosis made a difference in the type of medication the psychiatrist prescribed, and the boy functioned better after receiving the appropriate treatment.

Inattention and school failure can also be signs of depression or an anxiety disorder, and depression or anxiety can also result in impaired functioning on psychological tests that assess attention. The depressed or anxious child has to be differentiated from the ADHD child, and then there are also ADHD children who are depressed or anxious. In these latter cases, it is often difficult to determine to what extent the child's inattention is due to the ADHD and to what extent it is due to the depression or anxiety. Treating the depression or anxiety medically, and often with psychotherapy, can help ascertain what problems remain that might be attributed to ADHD.

It might also be true that a child who is reacting to stressful life situations, such as his parents' divorce or a parent's illness, can have problems concentrating in school, completing his work, and behaving appropriately. While it is often clear that these problems are not long-lasting enough to warrant a diagnosis of ADHD, there are children who react to chronic stress or to family conflict by developing long-standing depressive symptoms or more ingrained oppositional and defiant behavior, all of which might appear to be problems with attention and concentration. As with depression, there are also many children with ADHD who develop patterns of defiant behavior and who are oppositional to rules and authority. This behavior can exist along with ADHD.

One group of problems that can be especially difficult to differentiate from ADHD are learning disabilities. Children with ADHD and learning disabilities are often first identified in the same setting: school. This is because both conditions affect learning, and both interfere with the child's ability to function within the structure and the expectations of the school environment. While ADHD can cause difficulties in the child's attending to information in school and completing schoolwork and homework, the same can be true for learning disabilities. Children with learning disabilities that interfere with the processing of language will certainly miss important information that is spoken to them or that they read, and will certainly have problems completing their work efficiently.

Children with ADHD often have organizational problems as well. They cannot organize their backpacks, desks, notebooks, and folders. They often do their homework and fail to hand it in because they cannot find where they put it, or they did not place it where they can see it to remind them to hand it in. This problem is also common in children with nonverbal learning disabilities, which, by their nature, create problems with organization.

Not only do children with ADHD need to be distinguished from those with learning disabilities, but also we need to identify the large number of children who have both ADHD and learning disabilities, and determine how much of their problem is due to one or the other. This is important to be able to plan what sort of help to provide the child.

Children with pervasive developmental disorders might also have significant difficulty with attention regulation. These children have problems with intellectual, social, and emotional functioning that range from the more serious disorder of autism to the milder and less well defined Asperger's syndrome. Although many of these children might meet the diagnostic criteria for ADHD, their problems are more pervasive and affect a much wider area of functioning in their lives. Diagnosing them with ADHD does not provide the most complete explanation for their difficulties.

Differentiating among bipolar disorder, depression, situational reactions, oppositional defiant disorder, ADHD, learning disabilities, pervasive developmental disorders, or some combination of these problems is very important and can be very difficult.

Any diagnosis must be made by a qualified mental health or medical professional. A parent might want to see how many of the diagnostic criteria pertain to his or her child by the parent's observation. The parent should be reminded that the child functions in more than one setting and in the presence of people other than the parent. How the parent observes the child is one piece of evidence, and, however important the parent's perspective is, it might differ from the perspectives of others. The parent's impression by itself cannot determine whether or not the child has ADHD, but it can give the parent an idea about whether there is enough concern to pursue an evaluation further. To see if a child might fit the picture of ADHD, parents can take the symptom list (in Chapter 2) and rate their child on each symptom, as to how it compares to the typical child of that age. If the child has six or more frequently occurring symptoms in the inattention symptom group, or six or more frequently occurring symptoms in the hyperactivity-impulsivity symptom group, he has behavior that is consistent with at least one type of ADHD (Predominantly Inattentive Type or Predominantly Hyperactive-Impulsive Type). If he has six or more symptoms in *both* groups, his behavior is consistent with ADHD, Combined Type. If the parent can get someone else who knows the child well, such as a grandparent, to rate the child independently, this will provide additional information.

❖ CHAPTER 4 ❖

The Assessment Process

The assessment process begins with the parent's or teacher's impression that something is wrong. Sometimes the problem is obvious and sometimes it is subtle. It can be so subtle that it is not recognized by the parents or the school for years. Often, there are comments on the child's report card, dating back to early elementary school, that the child fails to complete his work, has missing homework assignments, is talkative in class, or has inconsistent effort or attention. If the child is hyperactive, these problems might be more obvious and bothersome to the teacher because they disrupt the normal flow of events in the classroom.

Have the parents received any of the following comments, in writing or verbally, from the child's teachers?

Incomplete assignments
Homework missing
Talkative
Not working to potential
Poor effort
Inconsistent effort
Doesn't pay attention

These are comments that parents of children with ADHD frequently receive over time. The persistence of these comments is an indication that there is something to be looked into more thoroughly.

If the child is not hyperactive and is relatively intelligent, these behaviors might be noticed but not be seen as serious because the child is not disruptive to the class and is not failing. Often the parents will be told that the child will "grow out of" the behavior, and that they should wait and see how the child does next year.

The assessment process is made confusing by several factors:

1. There is no one agreed-upon way to diagnose ADHD. There is no blood test or medical test that can identify ADHD. There is not even any reliable psychological test that can definitely rule in or rule out ADHD.
2. There are several professional disciplines that are generally considered to be qualified to diagnose ADHD. These professionals include psychologists, social workers, psychiatric nurses, mental health counselors, school psychologists, psychiatrists, neurologists, family physicians, and internists. They have widely different types of training and use very different methods to arrive at a diagnosis. Some rely solely on a patient's history and presenting complaints, some include a physical examination, some include psychological testing, and some use one or more of a variety of questionnaires or rating scales.
3. The diagnostic criteria for ADHD are not very specific. There are currently eighteen symptoms, or behaviors, in the *Diagnostic and Statistical Manual of Mental Disorders*, 4th edition (*DSM-IV*) that are used to determine if a person's functioning is consistent with ADHD (see Chapter 2). All of these symptoms include the word *often*, which is hard to quantify. The diagnostic criteria make it clear that these symptoms must be "maladaptive and inconsistent with developmental level," meaning that they have to occur more often than they do in the typical child of this age or stage of development. Still, what is too often for one family is quite tolerable for another.

Consider, for example, the symptom "often interrupts or intrudes on others." I grew up in an ethnic family in New York City, in which someone was always interrupting or intruding on someone else. But in New Hampshire, where I currently practice, many would find that degree of interruption intolerable.

4. There are several medical, neuropsychological, and psychiatric conditions that might look like ADHD. Inattention, impulsivity, and hyperactivity could be symptoms of a thyroid condition, lead poisoning, brain injury, learning disabilities, anxiety disorder, depression, and bipolar disorder, to name a few. These conditions should be considered and ruled out as probable causes of the child's behavior when a diagnosis of ADHD is being considered.
5. There are several conditions that might coexist with ADHD. The conditions mentioned in the above item can also coexist with ADHD, making it difficult to determine how much any particular symptom, such as inattention or fidgetiness, is due to ADHD or to the other condition.

Thus, there are many factors that must be considered in evaluating a child for ADHD. The evaluation, therefore, should be a comprehensive one and should consider all of these factors and conditions:

The length of time that the child has had these symptoms.

Whether the symptoms are significantly interfering with the child's functioning in important areas of life.

The child's medical and psychiatric history.

The child's developmental history (the mother's pregnancy, the child's birth, developmental milestones).

The family history.

Medical conditions that might look like ADHD.

Bipolar disorder (manic-depressive disorder).

Pervasive developmental disorders.

Anxiety disorder.

Depression.

Oppositional defiant disorder.

Conduct disorder.

Language-based learning disability.

Nonverbal learning disability.

Head injury.

A variation of normal behavior.

The current sources of stress in the child's and the family's life.

Early assessment and intervention are important, so as to preserve the child's self-esteem and positive attitude toward school, learning, and achievement. Too many parents who feel that there is something wrong feel put off by family, school personnel, or professionals who believe that they are overreacting to minor concerns. Years later, after many frustrating and wasted years in school, when the children who actually have ADHD are finally identified, many of these parents regret that help was not provided sooner.

It is also important that both parents participate in the assessment process and meet with the professionals who will be determining how their child is identified and influencing what services she will receive. It is not sufficient for one parent to leave it to the other to be the family's representative. Both parents, whether they are together or divorced, need to get the information directly from the source, and need to contribute their observations and insights to the information gathering. They need to be present to ask questions, express their doubts, and learn what they can do to help.

As an exercise, the clinician can ask each parent to list all of the school meetings and professional appointments that have been made in the past three years regarding their child's ADHD or related problems, and then indicate how many each has attended, and the percentage of the total meetings that this represents. Is each satisfied with his or her involvement? Is the spouse satisfied? Does the task of attending appointments fall on the mother because there is the assumption that this is the mother's role? If one parent is not satisfied with the other's lack of attendance at appointments, what goal do the parents need to set to increase their involvement?

Date and place of meeting	Attended	Did not attend

Percent of meetings I attended: ________%
Attendance goal for this year: ________%

Then they can begin to list the meetings for the coming year, and record their attendance:

Date and place of meeting	Attended	Did not attend

Attendance goal set for this year: ________%
Attendance goal achieved: ________%

Before the next school meeting, the parents can review the work that their child has brought home over the year, and read any evaluations that have been done on their child and any notes or comments from the teacher. They can make a list of their questions for the teacher or school team. The clinician can help the parents make this *their* meeting. They can take charge of the meeting rather than being passive recipients of the information that the school wants to give to them.

Our questions for the school

1.

2.

3.

4.

5.

The clinician can tell the parents that, when they go to the meeting, they should take notes on the responses they get to their questions and concerns, and they should indicate whether or not they are satisfied with the responses they receive and whether their questions are answered. They can take notes on any new information that is presented, and any concerns and questions they have about those new issues.

Problem we brought up	Response	Satisfied (S)/ dissatisfied (D)	Reasons for being (S) or (D)	New information	New questions and concerns

The parents will probably want to keep track of the modifications that the school is making for their child. This is particularly relevant if the child has an education plan, or if the school has promised to do certain things to help the child.

The parents can carry into the meetings a checklist of common modifications made for children with ADHD in school. The parent and the clinician can customize this list to the parents' needs. The clinician can copy this checklist, cross out the items that do not apply, and add others that do apply at the end:

Modifications

Have the child sit at the front of the classroom/close to the teacher/close to the blackboard.

Help the child break down his/her work into small units or "chunks."

Provide frequent praise.

Provide frequent short breaks from work and frequent opportunities for the child to check his/her work.

Develop and write down clearly defined behavioral goals.

Help the child break down long-term assignments into short-term or daily goals.

Reduce distractions for the student.

Allow the student the option of taking tests in a relatively distraction-free setting.

Allow the student to take tests in an untimed format.

Set clearly defined goals for behavior and task completion each day.

Actively engage the student through eye contact and verbal engagement.

Have the counselor help the student organize his/her papers and books, and check to see that all homework assignments are written down, on a daily basis.

Create a reward system with the use of points or tokens.

Supplement class lectures (auditory information) with visual information, such as written outlines of lectures.

Use colored highlighters to make work more visually stimulating.

Provide a written schedule.

Provide written behavioral expectations within plain sight of the student.

Provide a plan regarding where to go and whom to go to when the child is emotionally overwhelmed.

Have the child participate in a social skills group.

Provide a system of weekly feedback to the parents, either verbally or in writing.

Seat the child away from peers who might be distracting to him.

Paste a list of target behaviors on the child's desk.

Use touch and/or gentle verbal praise every 15 minutes when the child is on task.

Use touch and/or gentle verbal praise every 15 minutes when the child is behaving appropriately.

Similarly, for the child's next doctor's appointment, the parents can list their questions and concerns:

Questions for the next doctor's visit

1.

2.

3.

4.

As with the school meeting, the parents can record the doctor's responses, their level of satisfaction with them, and any new questions or concerns:

Problem we brought up	Response	Satisfied (S)/ dissatisfied (D)	Reasons for being (S) or (D)	New information	New questions and concerns

Each parent must be actively involved in providing information, getting information, and working with the professionals for the good of the child.

I often find that I have to help parents cope with their guilt for not having had their child evaluated sooner. Either they were not aware of the severity of the problem, or they were aware that something was wrong but they went along with the school in not being overly concerned at an earlier point in time. This guilt can be compounded by the parents' feelings about having pushed the child to do what he was unable to do; about having communicated to the child that he was not trying hard enough, didn't care, or was lazy; about not recognizing a problem earlier; or about knowing something was wrong but not taking forceful enough action in the face of resistance.

Parents often need to be educated about the ambiguity of ADHD, how it manifests itself differently in different children, and how children can compensate for this disorder and "get by" in school without sounding the alarm that there is a serious problem. Parents are dependent on the professionals in the child's life to help them sort out what might be wrong when things aren't going well. I have even seen trained mental health professionals overlook this disorder in their own children because it is often difficult to determine where personal characteristics and quirks end and an identifiable syndrome begins.

TESTING

Psychologists often use testing to clarify a diagnosis of ADHD and the nature and severity of the child's deficits. I often hear disagreement as to whether psychological testing is necessary to make a diagnosis of ADHD. It is important to understand that ADHD cannot be diagnosed on the basis of test results. There is no test that will definitively tell whether a child has or does not have ADHD. Even on tests that are supposedly sensitive to differentiating children with attention problems from children without attention problems, there are many children with ADHD who do well on these tests and many children without ADHD who do poorly.

So, a parent might ask, what is the usefulness of psychological testing? Psychological testing, like other forms of data gathering, such as school records, background information from the parents, and symptom questionnaires and rating scales, provides information that might be helpful for the clinician in judging whether or not a child has ADHD. Psychological testing provides some objective data about a child's performance on tasks that measure attention in various forms. Since other conditions, such as learning disabilities, might look like ADHD or coexist with ADHD, these objective data also provide information as to whether the child's problems might be wholly or partially due to these other conditions instead of ADHD.

Intelligence testing, which is often used in ADHD evaluations, also provides information about the child's skills in different types of learning, problem solving, and information processing. Comparing these skills to the child's attention on a variety of tasks can indicate whether his attention is deficient relative to his other cognitive abilities, or whether there are other cognitive deficiencies.

Achievement testing can indicate whether the child's academic skills are consistent with his intelligence, and whether or not attentional problems interfere with his performance on academic tasks. We often find that children with attention problems perform inconsistently on academic tasks, often failing relatively easy tasks and succeeding on more difficult ones, due to their wavering attention.

There are computerized tests, called continuous performance tests, that are used in ADHD assessments. Although often children with ADHD do well on them and children without ADHD do poorly, these tests provide laboratory measures of sustained attention and impulse control.

Psychologists also often make use of questionnaires and rating scales to be completed by the parents and the child's teachers. These forms might provide the psychologist with a description of the child's symptoms and problems, their severity, frequency, and in what situations they occur. Other scales provide normative information that statistically compares the child to other children his age across the country, to determine to what degree the child deviates from the norm on several characteristics of attention, behavior, and emotional difficulties. The ratings on these scales help to determine if the child deviates from the norm to a clinically significant degree and if there is an identifiable problem and not just a variation of normal behavior.

Psychological testing, therefore, is often an important component of a comprehensive assessment of ADHD. It provides useful information that must be considered with other sources of information in order to arrive at a picture of how the child is functioning.

In doing an assessment, I see myself as developing a "story" about the child. I am trying to develop a picture of how he is functioning in a way that helps explain his areas of difficulty and the variability that he experiences. It is not good enough to conclude that no problem has been found. Whatever comes up on the testing, the child is experiencing a problem. There has to be some way of explaining the child's difficulty whether or not he has ADHD. A good assessment has to recognize that there is a problem and address it in some way.

❖ CHAPTER 5 ❖

Identifying the Child's Problem Areas and Setting Goals

IDENTIFYING THE PROBLEMS

While children with ADHD might be united by a common group of symptoms, each of these children is truly unique. Each child has a different combination of symptoms, with different degrees of severity, varying in different situations. There are also situations in which the symptoms are not evident and the child does just fine. This is why ADHD is hard to diagnose. It can look very different in different children. Parents have at times reported that their child's teacher said that their child could not have ADHD because he or she was nothing like the other ADHD children they have had in their classes. Their child, for example, could sit still, whereas the ADHD children the teacher had known could not. Or, parents did not believe that their child had ADHD because he was not "bouncing off the walls" and "destroying the house" like the ADHD child who lived next door.

Another consideration is that the symptoms listed in the diagnostic criteria are very general and do not mention the specific behaviors of any one child. For example, nowhere in the diagnostic criteria are the following listed: "pulls cereal boxes down from the shelves in the supermarket," or "acts like a maniac whenever his brother is around."

Describing a specific ADHD child involves a lot more than referring to the diagnostic criteria. It involves the intimate knowledge of a child that only a parent can provide. The first step in solving a problem is identifying it. The clinician can help the parents identify the child's specific problem areas, how often they occur, and how severe they are, so that the parents can better communicate with professionals about their child.

Now the parents might have a better sense of the types of problems that their child has—a little more specific detail than just "he drives me crazy," or "he's always in trouble." Since it would probably be impossible and overwhelming to concern themselves equally with all of these problems all of the time, the parents can now consider which are most important to focus their energies on, and which they can choose to let go of for now. In the next section, they will have the opportunity to define those concerns that they want to make the focus of their attention and their work. They should keep these problem areas in mind as they set the goals for themselves.

Problem	Where does this occur? How often? (1 = Seldom, 2 = Sometimes, 3 = Frequently)	How severe is this problem? (1 = Mild, 2 = Moderate, 3 = Severe)
Does not pay attention		
Forgets things		
Doesn't finish work		
Disorganized		
Doesn't listen		
Doesn't sit still		
Interrupts		
Doesn't wait turn		
Peer problems		
Homework problems		
Aggressive		
Easily frustrated		
Emotions out of control		
Poor self-esteem		
Oppositional/defiant		
Distracted		
Aggressive		
Takes too long to do things		
Restless or fidgety		
Can't stay seated		
Loses things		
Runs around/climbs on things		
Too noisy or talkative		
Bossy with peers or siblings		
Difficulty following rules		
Talks too much		
Silly or inappropriate		
Angry often		
Poor sense of personal space		

SETTING GOALS

For parents to get the most out of their work with the clinician, they should set goals for themselves. The clinician should ask them to think about what they want to accomplish, what they want to do better, and what they would like to help their child do better. By setting these goals, they will be better able to apply the exercises in this book to their specific needs, keep track of their progress, and identify obstacles. As they go along, the parents can modify their goals or add new ones as their understanding of themselves and their child improves.

In helping the parents list their goals, the clinician should keep in mind the problem areas they defined in the previous chapter, as well as things that they could improve in their own behavior, including things they do by themselves (such as make more time for leisure activities), things they do with their child (such as be more patient or yell less), or things they do with their spouse (such as ask for help more or give feedback in a kinder way).

LISTING GOALS

As a first step, the parents can make a brainstorming list. To do this, they should write down, without editing, as it comes to mind, anything that they would like to improve. Anything that comes to mind should be written down, no matter how unrealistic, silly, impossible, or embarrassing it might seem. They should not censor or organize the list yet.

My brainstorming list

Now the parents should organize their lists by the types of goals, finding things that the goals have in common. Some categories to consider are:

Goals to manage my child's behavior better

Goals to communicate better with my spouse or ex-spouse

Goals to control my own behavior and emotions better

Goals to manage my time and activities better

Goals to decrease stress

The clinician can add other categories, but should try to limit the number of categories to keep the list manageable.

My brainstorming list with headings

Goal type #1	Goal type #2	Goal type #3	Goal type #4

Now that each parent has several categories, it might help them to think of additional related goals and add them to their lists. Next, the parents look over their lists and try to make their goals as specific as possible, putting them in terms that describe specific behaviors that they can observe or change. For example, if one goal for their child is "cooperate better," that might translate into "do what he is told to do, the first time, within 30 seconds, without an argument." If a personal goal is "communicate better with my husband (or wife)," it might be more specific as "offer my opinion gently and calmly without being judgmental, and by listening to his/her response without butting in."

PRIORITIZING

Next, prioritize the goals. Each parent can take a colored highlighter and highlight one goal from each category that he or she would like to work on first. In considering which goals to choose, the parents should think about which goals are specifically defined so as to be easily measurable, and capable of being accomplished in a relatively short period of time. It is important that they start off doing something they have a realistic chance of accomplishing in a brief period of time, in order to give them an experience of success. This will also reinforce them for identifying their goals in ways that allow them to see what they have to do to change, and allow them to clearly see the changes when they occur.

IDENTIFYING THEIR STRENGTHS AND WEAKNESSES

Critical to meeting goals is what parents bring to the table—their own strengths and weaknesses. It helps for parents to be honest with themselves. They can ask themselves: Am I empathic? firm? rigid? authoritative? a pushover? inconsistent? loving? Often it helps to get feedback from others who know them well and have observed them with their child. This feedback might be different from the way they like to think of themselves. The clinician can coach the parents to consider each person's input as possibly having merit, rather than being defensive about it, and to be open-minded as to whether it is true. They might learn something new about themselves, or find out whether they have good reasons to see things differently than others do.

Often, a parent's strengths are counterbalanced by weaknesses. For example, a parent might be firm and structured, but not sufficiently warm and empathic. Conversely, a parent might be endowed with an abundance of nurturance, but be poor at asserting authority. One might intervene in problems quickly, but might lack patience. Or one might have a great deal of patience, but might negotiate with his child for too long.

The parents can make a list of their strengths, based on their own perceptions of themselves and the opinions of others who know them. When they are finished listing these attributes in the left-hand column, they should determine if there are any corresponding weaknesses, and list them in the right-hand column. Not all strengths will necessarily have a corresponding weakness. If there are additional weaknesses, they can list them in the right-hand column.

Strengths	Weaknesses

Now the parents can look back at their priorities. They can take one goal and imagine a situation in which they would try to achieve this goal. For example, if their goal is to get their child to do what he or she is told to do without a tantrum, they might imagine a specific situation, such as bedtime. It might help for them to sit in a comfortable chair at home, close their eyes, and visualize the situation. First, they can visualize it as it usually goes, when it is frustrating to them. Next, they can imagine it going the way they would prefer it, with both they and their child doing things differently to change the situation.

After visualizing the better situation, they can write down this restructured scenario in detail. It is useful to take the time to do this, as writing helps them to remember all the details, and also helps them to fill in additional ideas that they think of while they are writing.

Next, they can look over their list of strengths and weaknesses. Which of their strengths come into play in making the situation better?

Are there strengths that they are not using?

Which of their weaknesses are getting in the way?

For example, a parent might imagine going upstairs with the child and telling the child that it is time to get into his pajamas and brush his teeth. The child ignores the parent's command, and the parent then tells the child to look at him, gives the child the command again, and tells the child the consequence that he will experience (such as time-out, or loss of quiet play time before bed) if he does not comply right away. The parent can then imagine the child complying. The parent can take note of the following:

How did you imagine feeling each step of the way?

Were there any points at which you felt frustrated?

How did you imagine handling your frustration? Was it in a way that would or would not escalate into a control struggle?

When you were frustrated, did you talk to yourself, telling yourself to calm down? Did you ask your spouse to take over for a minute?

Were there points at which you felt pleased with your child's response? Did you praise your child at those points?

In what ways were you pleased with yourself? Did you tell yourself that you did a good job?

Now the parent can visualize the situation again, employing his strengths and correcting for his weaknesses. He will see that it is not only the child or the spouse who has to change to make him a more effective parent. The parent can ask himself: Were there points at which I could have been more authoritative? More flexible? Negotiated more? Negotiated less? Asked for help? Left the room? Praised more? To continue this exercise, the parent can write down the newly restructured scenario:

The next time this situation comes up (for the example, this would be the next night when the parents put their child to bed), they can recall the visualization just before bedtime, and keep it in mind as they go through the steps of putting the child to bed. They should pay attention to what goes the way it was envisioned and what does not. Then they can write down how it went and what else has to change, in themselves or in the child to bring the situation closer to the way they want it to be.

How the situation went:

What has to change:

Now that the parents have a better idea of the child's difficulties, what they would like to change, and the strengths and weaknesses that they and the rest of the family bring to the situation, it helps to develop an action plan to map out the changes that the parents want to make. An action plan also specifies the time by which the parents want to accomplish the changes. It can combine both short-term and long-term goals. The parents can start with goals that can realistically be accomplished within the next month. It would be a mistake just to go with goals that the parents want to accomplish right away. They need to be realistic about how soon they will be able to accomplish the goals. They can write these goals down and set realistic dates. Then they can break each of these goals into smaller steps that describe more immediate actions they can take on the way to this goal. For example, the parents' goal might be:

Have Fred complete his bedtime routine cooperatively, and with our remaining calm, by Friday, April 24.

Then, the parents can break down the goal into more immediate steps:

Main goal: Cooperative and calm bedtime routine by Friday, April 24.

1. Write down the sequence of behaviors that Fred is expected to do in his bedtime routine, and have it double checked by spouse, by Monday, April 20.

2. Decide with spouse on the consequence of Fred's not complying by being ready for bed by 9 p.m. (such as decreased time for reading), by Monday, April 20.

3. Decide with spouse on signals to use when one of us needs relief before losing our cool, by Monday, April 20.

4. Review the sequence of behaviors with Fred, the intent to have him in bed by 9 p.m., and the consequences of not complying, by Tuesday, April 21.

5. Have "practice runs" of the new routine to provide Fred with familiarity with the new expectations, to provide me with practice in keeping my cool, and to provide me and my spouse practice with communicating when we need relief, on Wednesday and Thursday, April 22 and 23.

6. Implement the system on Friday, April 24.

The action plan can then list all of the parents' goals and their steps in the order in which they will be accomplished:

My action plan

Main Goal	Date Due	Steps	Date Due
Calm and cooperative bedtime routine	Friday, April 24		
		1. Write down sequence and check with spouse	April 20
		2. Establish consequence for noncompliance	April 20
		3. Decide on signals with spouse for relief	April 20
		4. Review the plan and consequences with Fred	April 21
		5. Practice runs	April 22 and 23
		6. Implement	April 24

❖ CHAPTER 6 ❖

Discipline and Authority

The exercises in this chapter are designed to help parents understand how they use authority and how they can use it more productively.

AUTHORITY

Parents can begin this examination of their styles of authority by asking themselves: What kind of an authority am I? Do I control my children with a firm hand? Do I let my children run all over me? Do I feel guilty about how I punish my kids? Do I lose control because I feel that my children are controlling me? Do I negotiate too much? Do I refuse to negotiate at all?

Parents need to see that authority comes in different forms. The clinician can explain the task this way: "It might help to understand what kind of authority you and your spouse are, how compatible you are with each other, and whether or not it is good for the children."

There are several aspects to authority that have been found to be good for children. There should be a clear *hierarchy* in the family. That is, parents should be in charge, they should be recognized as such, and they should be accorded respect. A family is not a democracy. While parents can respect the opinions and the feelings of the children, the children need to know that the ultimate decisions about family life are made by the parents, and that parents and children are unequal in power. For example, many parents believe that their children's opinions should be solicited and listened to. They believe, with good reason, that this can help build better self-esteem and verbal skills in children. However, this philosophy should not be used as an excuse for the parents to give up their decision-making responsibilities. The children might weigh in with their opinions about where to go on vacation, whether or not to move, which car to buy, or what to do on Saturday, but they should also know that the final decisions about family life are the responsibility of the parents.

Along similar lines, parents might value their children's right to express their feelings, even if these feelings are not pleasant for the parents. However, there is a difference between having a feeling and expressing it in a respectful way. Children who express their anger in ways that are inappropriate or disrespectful are not being taught that their feelings are valuable; they are being taught that they do not have to follow rules and respect authority, and that they cannot both disagree with and respect someone.

Enforcing the hierarchy in the family does not mean that authority should be wielded in harsh, punitive, or threatening ways. It is also important for the children to receive *nurturance* from their parents. Parents need to be in charge *and* to be warm and loving. It does not weaken the parents' authority to be loving, warm, and understanding toward their children, or to solicit their opinions and feedback. In fact, it is those parents who are most secure in their authority who feel that they can ask their children's opinion, and even change their minds out of respect for their children's opinion, without losing their authority in their own eyes or those of their children.

Authority should also be *goal-oriented*. Discipline should have direction. Children should not be punished arbitrarily, just so the parents can assert their authority. Punishment should not be so inconsistent that it is confusing to the child, for example, punishing him severely for a minor infraction one day and then not responding to a major violation another day. Discipline should seem to make sense to both parent and child. Even if the child does not like the discipline, he should be able to predict what types of behavior will get him punished and with what severity.

Discipline should be rooted in the values of the parents. Underlying any discipline should be the parents' sense of what kind of child they want to develop. This means that if the parents value respect, then respectful behavior on the part of the child will be rewarded, disrespectful behavior will be punished, and this will be done consistently.

The parents should be secure enough in their authority to allow for communication within the family. Allowing children to question, protest, and negotiate, and listening to them, should not be experienced as threatening to the parents as long as these expressions are appropriate and respectful of the hierarchy in the family.

Parents generally find that they fit into one of three types of authority styles: authoritative, authoritarian, or permissive. *Authoritative* parents establish a firm and clear hierarchy in the family. The parents are the unquestioned bosses in the family. At the same time, they are open to discussing matters with their children and they are able to provide nurturance and praise. Authoritative parents also tend to be goal-oriented. Their discipline makes sense and sends a consistent message about values and consequences. In addition, the child can count on the fact that the type of consequence will be predictable (such as time-out, or the loss of a privilege) and fair. There will not be lax discipline one day and overly harsh or cruel discipline the next. Discipline will reflect the parents' values, such as the idea that children should be treated with firmness, but with respect for their safety and without verbal or physical cruelty. Authoritative parenting has been clearly shown to promote healthier self-esteem in children and better spousal relationships.

Authoritarian parents are clearly in charge and tolerate no discussion or challenge in any way. Their control is so complete that any discussion is seen as subversive. Praise and nurturance are rarely used and are often regarded as signs of weakness by the parent. The children's opinions are not solicited because they are seen as challenges to the parents' authority. Authoritarian parenting puts the parents in control, with a very clear hierarchy and clear goals. However, the lack of nurturance and the intolerance of discussion promote oppositional and defiant behavior and lower self-esteem in children, more spousal dissatisfaction, and less identification with the parent when the child is older. The intolerance and inflexibility inherent in this style suggest that authoritarian parenting is actually based on a foundation of insecurity in the parent rather than on confidence.

Permissive parenting does not provide the hierarchy that promotes positive behavior, respect for authority, or the ability to respect rules that children need in order to feel safe and secure in the world. It is parenting without goals, restrictions, or demands. Permissive parents often feel that they have to be the child's "friend" first. The children are treated as the parents' equals in authority, a situation that denies the real differences between adults and children, and removes the adults' responsibility for caregiving. The parents might be warm, empathic, and flexible to the point of ineffectiveness. Discussion is tolerated at the expense of authority. The parents are simply not doing their jobs.

Answering the following questions, and getting feedback from one's spouse, might help parents see what kind of authority they are:

Do I have clear lines of authority? Am I definitely "the boss"? (hierarchical)

Am I specific about what I want my child to do when I tell him to do something, rather than using general or vague commands? (goal-oriented)

Do I refuse to change my commands under any circumstances, once I give them? (authoritarian)

Do I often change my commands and give in? (permissive)

Do I refuse to discuss discipline with my child? (authoritarian)

Does my spouse feel that I discuss things too much or for too long with my child? (permissive)

Can I express warmth to my child even when I am angry? (nurturing)

Do I believe that being warm and loving will undermine my authority? (authoritarian)

Do I praise my child often? (nurturing)

Do I praise my child for special things (such as cleaning up when he is not supposed to)? (nurturing)

Do I praise my child for everyday good behavior? (nurturing)

Does my child ever question my authority? How do I react?

- Do I listen, as long as my authority is not being undermined at the moment, but remain in charge? (authoritative)
- Do I always refuse to listen and always feel that my authority is being undermined? (authoritarian)
- Do I always listen, even when my child is undermining my authority at the moment he is challenging me? (permissive)
- Do I tolerate prolonged interactions in which my child is disrespectful, rather than responding immediately with a clear limit? (permissive)

Am I frequently punishing my children? (authoritarian)

Are my punishments excessive and extreme? (authoritarian)

The parents can then fill in the following table of types of discipline and their effectiveness:

Discipline	**Frequency:**	**Effectiveness:**
	(4) more than once a day	(4) very effective: works most of the time
	(3) once a day	(3) somewhat effective: works half the time
	(2) several times a week	(2) not too effective: works less than half the time
	(1) once a week or less	(1) ineffective: hardly ever works
Time out		
Yelling		
Spanking		
Praising good behavior		
Point system		

Since none of us is completely objective when assessing our own behavior, the parent can have someone who knows him and his household well review the chart. If the spouse is in the home, she can give him feedback. One of the children might also be a good source of feedback.

Feedback about discipline

After considering this input, the parent can modify the chart as needed. Now that the parent sees what methods he uses, how often he uses them, and whether they are effective, he can look at the methods that are ineffective or that he does not feel good about using.

If a method is ineffective, there could be a problem with the method itself or with how the parent is using it. Parents often tell me very matter-of-factly, "Oh, we use "time-out," when I ask them what they do for discipline. When I ask them to describe in detail what actually occurs during time-out, I get a wide variety of stories. They tell the child to get into the time-out area, only to have him resist. They then might pick the child up and carry him to the time-out area, while arguing and yelling at the child, and with the child yelling back. Or they will engage in a verbal shouting match with the child as he resists but eventually complies. When the child is seated in the time-out chair, many parents report that he is continually turning to them or shouting to them from the other room to ask them if the time-out is over or when it will end. Often, the argument that started before the time-out was implemented, or while it was being carried out, just continues from the time-out chair, with the parent participating.

Time-out is supposed to be *time-out from reinforcement*. Reinforcement is anything that follows a behavior and increases the likelihood of that behavior continuing. Generally, getting into a control struggle with the child, engaging in conversation about when time-out will end, or looking over and making eye contact when the child is screaming from the time-out chair reinforces him for that negative behavior. It gives the child attention and the upper hand in a control struggle, and provides stimulation, engagement, and social interaction when he is supposed to be deprived of all these things. So, parents might think that they are punishing the child and that they are using time-out, but they are not!

Before parents can decide that time-out is ineffective, they have to learn how to use it. If the child's negative behavior keeps happening, it is probably being reinforced, even if the parents think they are punishing it. Therefore, if the parents tell the child to go to the time-out area, and the parents get into an argument with the child about it, or if they persist in reminding him to go, or telling him to calm down, or answering his questions, then the child's behavior is probably being reinforced by the parents' interaction with him. If the child succeeds in involving the parents in any interaction whatsoever, the child is in control of the situation. Once the child is in time-out, he might persist in trying to get the parent's attention. If the parent speaks to, or even makes eye contact with the child, the parent is reinforcing the child's negative behavior.

When threatened with deprivation, a child will try to engage the parents in some form of interaction, which gives him a sense of control. A child in time-out should have no interaction or stimulation. So, to enforce *real* time-out, I suggest the following to parents:

1. Pick a place that is away from distractions, where your child cannot interact with anyone, play with toys, or view the television or family activity. Usually, the child's room is not the best place for a time-out (although it might do nicely for a place in which to cool down and get away from the heat of an interaction) because there are too many fun things to do in there.
2. Tell your child that he has to go into time-out for a specified period of time (such as five minutes), and that you will tell him when it is time to come out. Tell him that he can only come out if he has calmed down. Tell your child you will not speak to him during this time, and that if he persists in asking you when he can come out, you will add time onto his time-out.
3. If your child does not go into time-out, and he is of a size where it is safe and appropriate to physically control him, gently but firmly escort him into time-out. When you do this, act as if you were a robot that you had programmed to take this action. Make no eye contact and have no verbal interaction whatsoever. Do not hold your child more tightly out of anger. Do not plead, beg, threaten, respond to, or otherwise engage your child. Do not answer questions.

4. If you cannot physically force your child into time-out, have significant consequences you can impose that you do control.
5. While your child is in time-out, ignore him. If he gets out of the time-out chair or room, gently but firmly bring him back to it, as you were instructed above.
6. When the time-out is over, calmly tell your child that he can come out. If he was placed in time-out for refusing to do something, tell him to do it now, or put him back into time-out.

The parent can use this list as a checklist and have his spouse observe him enforcing a time-out. She can check off the things that he does effectively as well as critique the things that he should be doing differently, to be communicated to him at a later time.

If the parents change their tactics and implement a firm and consistent time-out procedure, such as outlined above, their child might resist at first. In fact, his negative and defiant behavior might escalate. This does not mean that the child's negative behavior is being reinforced by them. If they were doing the same thing time and again and got the same response from their child, then they were probably reinforcing the behavior. In the case of using time-out more consistently, the child's initial resistance is to be expected. The parents' response should be to continue to be firm and consistent, to stick with it, and to counter the child's testing with their unyielding response until the child understands that his behavior will not change things.

PRAISING GOOD BEHAVIOR

Children with ADHD receive much negative feedback for what they do wrong. We want to increase the times in which they are quietly doing what we normally expect a child to do, for example, cooperating and taking turns while playing with siblings or peers, sitting quietly at the dinner table and politely participating in the conversation, and waiting their turn in conversations or play activities. To do this, we have to make the simple, good things that they do as much of an "event" as the negative things about which we make such a fuss. It is through direct praise, repeated immediately following the behavior, and frequently over time, that the child learns the behavior that we value and makes it a part of himself. Therefore, it is important for parents to train themselves to deliver this praise frequently throughout the day, even every fifteen minutes or so on some occasions, when the child is behaving in a way that the parent desires. Praise should be specific. It should be clear to the child specifically what behavior you are praising. If your child is sitting quietly, and you just say, "You're doing great," it might be obvious to you what you are praising, but your child might be thinking about hitting his brother or blowing up the house! So, to avoid any of this sort of misunderstanding, it would be better to say, "I'm very proud of you. You are sitting quietly, and letting other people talk."

Praise should also be frequent. The ADHD child needs continual positive reinforcement for good behavior. This is how his brain is "fed." Frequent positive reinforcement helps to counteract the large number of negative comments that these children experience, and corrects the balance so the child is getting more positive feedback than negative. It is not good enough to tell the child what he is not supposed to do, but he must also be instructed in what he *is* supposed to do. The greatest effect on a child's behavior is exercised by the event that immediately follows the behavior. Therefore, immediate positive reinforcement will make it most likely that the behavior will happen again.

REFRAINING FROM YELLING OR SPANKING

Yelling and spanking are usually the parents' response to their own frustration, rather than well thought out, rational methods of discipline. When parents yell, it might frighten a child, but it might also give a child a feeling of control over the parents' emotional state. I have seen children tolerate physical punishment and deprivation of privileges in order to stay in an interaction with an angry parent. Once parents yell, the child has succeeded in controlling them and they have lost an important component of their authority.

Spanking inflicts physical hurt on a child and teaches him that "might makes right," rather than "what's right makes right." It is important for parents to learn ways to be effective authorities and to use their leverage without resorting to physical punishment. As one parent told her aggressive ADHD child: "If you hit your sister, you give her permission to hit you." The same can be said for hitting your child. If a parent hits a child, the parent is modeling that hitting is an acceptable reaction to anger and frustration.

Parents are powerful models to children. The old saying, "Do what I say, not what I do," just doesn't work. The child is more likely to end up doing what the parent does. Since many children with ADHD are impulsive and have difficulty controlling their aggression, ingraining in them the experience that this behavior is acceptable is a dangerous thing.

HELPING PARENTS TRACK CHANGES IN THEIR PARENTING STYLE

If the goal is to become more effective in the authoritative style of parenting, it might help the parent to chart his changes so there can be visible evidence of progress over time. The parent can list the characteristics of authoritative and nonauthoritative (authoritarian or permissive) parenting, and mark off how often he uses each during the week. The parent can go over it every day with his spouse, too, as a reality check. He can also provide the same reality check for his spouse:

Week of ____________________

Authoritative methods	Frequency	Non-authoritative methods	Frequency
Praising good behavior immediately		Spanking	
Time-out		Yelling	
Immediate consequences		Backing down	
Point system		Undermining spouse	
Specific commands		Losing control of anger	
Praise for everyday good behavior		Refusing to listen to child	
		Refusing to change even when it is in everyone's best interest	
		Negotiating too much	

DIFFERENCES BETWEEN FATHERS AND MOTHERS

Fathers and mothers have many complaints about each other that come up repeatedly in my practice. While I don't wish to stereotype people according to their sex, these trends are too common not to notice. I also find that what each spouse complains about as a problem in the other parent can also be used as a strength.

We often view things as problems merely because they differ from the way that we see and do things. It is often hard to see how these differences can complement what we have to offer and make us more effective. For example, I often see parents polarized along the lines of who is too strict and who is too lenient. I more commonly hear mothers accusing fathers of being too strict, and fathers accusing mothers of being too lenient.

Fathers often take a businesslike approach to discipline. They tend to think linearly, seeing the shortest distance between two points (undesirable behavior and its consequences) as a straight line (immediate, non-negotiable punishment). They often feel that mothers spend too much time and energy negotiating with and feeling sorry for their children, and therefore being manipulated by them into delaying or softening punishment. They often believe that the child's displays of emotion are not signs of genuine distress, but rather are attempts at manipulation. Since they see the mothers as "softies," they might, in reaction, become stricter and harsher.

Mothers, on the other hand, often feel that fathers are too strict and that they fail to respond to or understand the child's emotional needs. They feel that this neglect of the child's sensitivities is harmful to the child and actually makes discipline less effective. While fathers might see emotions as distractions on the road to consequences, to mothers they are the very heart and soul of family life. Therefore, getting from point A to point B often takes a circuitous route, which, from this point of view, is the way it should be. Negotiating with the child leads to greater emotional understanding and consequences that everyone can live with. Mothers often feel that fathers ignore signs of genuine emotional distress in their children.

Therefore, we have a setup for a conflict between mothers, who often are more emotionally in tune or empathic with their children, tend to negotiate more, and respond to their child's negative emotions as signs of genuine distress, and fathers, who often impose more demands on their children regardless of the child's wishes, discipline in a more businesslike way, put emotions on the back burner, and view the child's emotional displays as manipulative.

One word of caution, however, is in order. Although fathers often view mothers as too involved in the emotional interchanges with their children, there is one emotion about which I often find fathers totally irrational. That emotion is anger. I often find that fathers become irrationally angry when a child challenges their authority. Although being an authority is just as important to mothers as it is to fathers, fathers see authority as being part of the very core of their being. Men tend to see the world in terms of hierarchy, that is, who has power, control, and authority. That's why men are notorious for being unwilling to stop and ask for directions when they are driving. They would rather drive around lost for hours, fooling themselves that they can find their way, rather than be in a one-down position. These same men, by contrast, will go out of the way to give someone directions or other help. Being the expert puts them in a position of authority. Women, on the other hand, try to put themselves into the experience of others, to make themselves equal in status to the people with whom they are relating.

In relationships in which a man is supposed to be in charge, there can be no negotiation. Therefore, a child's affront to the father's authority shakes the father's very foundation, and makes objectivity impossible. Fathers strive so desperately to assert their authority for its own sake that they can be blind to whether they are engaging their child in a control struggle that actually undermines their authority.

These differences are explored in detail in the excellent book by Dr. Deborah Tannen (1990), *You Just Don't Understand*. Although these differences are common, they do not describe all fathers and mothers, or any father or mother all the time.

It would be useful to see how these tendencies fit the parents through their self-examination. Once parents recognize that there are common tendencies to how we see the world, based on our experiences of being men or women in the world, they can be freed up to see that their perspective is relative and not the only truth, and that there is a lot they can learn from their spouses. Therefore, recognizing stereotypes, and how they might be true, can be a first step to overcoming them.

Parents can ask themselves these questions, and see if their spouses confirm their perspective:

1. If your children cry when being disciplined, do you always dismiss these tears as being manipulative? ________
2. Do you always see these tears as signs of distress and feel sorry for the child and/or guilty for disciplining her? ________

3. Do you ever discuss your child's feelings with her, without giving her advice or telling her what to do? ________
4. Do you ever sit and observe your child playing without commenting or joining in? ________
5. Do you let your child take the lead in play and tell you what to do? ________
6. Do you ever see negotiating your limits with your child as being useful? ________
7. Are you consistently inconsistent in your discipline because your child always gets upset? ________
8. Do you lose control of the disciplinary situation when you get angry? ________
9. When you play with your child, do you usually take the lead or introduce new themes? ________
10. When you discuss your child's feelings with her, do you usually give advice and find it hard just to listen without recommending a course of action? ________
11. Are you intolerant of questions from your child about limits and consequences? ___________
12. Do you often find yourself suspending your discipline or limit setting because you want to understand or alleviate your child's hurt feelings?

"Yes" answers to questions 1, 8, 9, 10, and 11 indicate a typically male perspective, and "yes" answers to questions 2, 3, 4, 5, 6, 7, and 12 indicate a typically female perspective.

It is important to understand that we all have different perspectives based on who we are, apart from our objective understanding of the situation or our ability to see the whole truth. Our perspectives lead us to see the evidence that supports our view of the world and dismiss evidence that does not support how we view things. Appreciating one's spouse's perspective will help a parent to see evidence that he or she might have overlooked or devalued, and therefore help the parent to be more objective.

CHILDREN AS "LAWYERS"

Some very bright children with ADHD become masterful at using words and marshaling logic to support their causes. A parent might find himself in frequent arguments with his 5-year-old, justifying and rationalizing his punishments, rules, or limits, against an intensely vociferous argument to the contrary. Rather than behave in a directly defiant and oppositional manner, the child has instead learned to use adult-like logic and reason to prolong the interaction with the parent, delay or even end the imposition of consequences, and engage the parent in a control struggle on the parent's own terms. This is a sneaky and indirect way of being oppositional and defiant that some children are good at because they are only asking for an explanation and justification of the parent's actions.

Parents who believe that they owe it to their child to explain everything and to get their child's agreement or approval are particularly susceptible to this type of manipulation. Children with coexisting oppositional defiant disorder are particularly susceptible to engaging their parents in this type of interchange.

If a parent believes he owes his child an explanation for his actions, or that his child benefits from such an explanation, this is fine and can be helpful. But after the explanation is given once, providing the explanation a second time or more is only getting trapped in a control struggle with the child. I often ask parents who repeatedly justify their actions if they have any reason to believe that their child's intelligence is not normal, or that their child has reached an age of senility. If the answers to these questions are no, then repeating themselves is not providing the child with any new information. It is merely prolonging the disciplinary interaction and delaying the implementation of discipline, leaving the child in control. Since the child is in control in these prolonged, exasperating, legalistic interactions, the behavior is self-reinforcing for the child. The parent does not have to explain his actions to the child's satisfaction or to meet with the child's approval. Once is enough.

The clinician might ask a parent who is prone to being put on the witness stand by his child to keep track of how many explanations he gives his child for each limit or consequence that he imposes. He can chart it like this:

Disciplinary Event	Number of explanations

The goal is simple: get the number of explanations down to one per incident.

RESPECT FOR AUTHORITY

Many parents tolerate blatant acts of disrespect from their children in order to keep the peace and not have one more thing to wage a battle over. Some children with ADHD are so intense a management problem that the disrespectful things they say or do to their parents often are no longer noticed by the parent. They become part of the background and are not as important as the major rule violations that the parent is dealing with. I believe that ignoring a child's disrespectful behavior is a big mistake. These types of behaviors include the following:

The child calls the parent "stupid" or "dumb" or something even worse (the parent might be so accustomed to hearing worse names from the child that "stupid" or "dumb" does not sound so bad).

The child sticks his tongue out at the parent.

The child mimics or mocks the parent's words or facial expressions.

The child raises his voice to the parent.

The child uses a tone of voice that he would use with a peer.

The child talks over the parent.

The child throws something at the parent.

The child uses obscene language.

These behaviors must be responded to immediately and firmly with a time-out or a consequence. Parents might need help in understanding why this is a major, and not a minor, issue. If a child acts or speaks disrespectfully to an authority figure, it puts the child on an equal or superior footing to that authority figure. If the child is allowed to get away with this, no matter how effective the parent is in setting limits, the child will not develop a healthy respect for authority. This can lead to the attitude, later in life, that he does not have to listen to or obey anybody, and that other people are being unreasonable. This can result in adjustment problems in most areas of life. Since parents might not even notice this behavior, it would help them to attend to it. They can do this informally, or through a written record such as this:

Disrespectful behavior	Week 1	Week 2	Week 3
Calling parent a name			
Using an obscenity			
Disrespectful gesture (sticking out tongue, hand gesture)			
Mimicking or mocking			
Raising voice			
Inappropriate tone of voice			
Talking over			
Throwing object			

The parent might be surprised at how often he or she permits this inappropriate behavior to occur without a response. The parent can now monitor the behavior with a zero tolerance for disrespect.

KEEPING AWAY FROM CONTROL STRUGGLES

Most parents get sucked in to control struggles with their children, at least some of the time. Much of the advice and many of the techniques in this book are designed to eliminate these control struggles. This is a subject that comes up often with parents of children with ADHD. Control struggles can be so insidious that often the parent just believes he is asserting his authority, without realizing that his authority has been lost—it has been given away to his child. Then it takes much more work to get it back.

Control struggles are any prolonged interactions in which the limits or behavioral expectations are delayed, refused, or ignored by the child despite the persistent effort of the parent to enforce the limit or expectation. The parent might argue, remind, threaten, cajole, beg, plead, punish, scream at, or debate the child, but the interaction continues without resolution, at least for longer than the parent wants it to. During this struggle, no matter how long it lasts, the child has control over the parent. Even if the parent eventually gets his way, the child's control over the parent, for whatever period of time it lasts, is a victory, and is thus reinforcing for the child's oppositional behavior. Therefore, it is important to teach parents that if they are engaging in control struggles with their child they are losing the war even if they win some battles.

To circumvent control struggles, I try to help parents intervene sooner rather than later, and abbreviate the amount of time they spend interacting with their child during discipline or limit setting. This might involve limiting the number of warnings the parent gives to the child, especially if the parent has gone over a particular behavior repeatedly and the child is well aware of the parent's behavioral expectations. It might also involve physically removing the child from the situation and placing him in time-out or in the child's room, immediately after the child fails to comply with a parental command to do just that.

Parents also tend to get drawn into control struggles when their children argue against the logic of their punishments or ask for the reasons for them. The guideline here is consistent with other advice on control struggles—keep interactions to a minimum. Offer an explanation or reason only once, if you must, and then enforce the limit, refusing further discussion.

Some children engage in the wild technique of throwing and banging things in their room and opening their door to "escape" when they are put in there. This can force the parent to respond verbally, by talking through the door to the child, or to respond physically, by engaging in a tug-of-war with the child to keep the door closed, or visually, by making eye contact each time the child opens the door. The parent in this case should only intervene when safety is an issue, and should do so nonverbally and without eye contact, by simply restraining the child or removing objects from the room when necessary. The parent can also maintain firm pressure on the door handle to keep the door shut, and try to prevent the door from opening and closing so the child can't periodically poke his head out. Ignoring the child while enforcing the limit is the rule.

INEFFECTIVE AUTHORITY

There are many types of ineffective authority. Although this list is worded in a negative way, it can serve as an effective reminder of what parents might do to undermine themselves without thinking:

Threaten what you won't follow through on.

Explain your reasons to your child more than once.

Yell and scream louder than your child.

Handle your child aggressively.

Plead, beg, and cajole your child to do something.

End your commands with the question: "OK?" ("You have to put the toys away now, OK?").

Don't check with your spouse before changing a rule, expectation, or punishment.

Set punishments to last for several weeks.

Let your child off a punishment for good behavior.

Set a consequence for a certain behavior inconsistently.

Argue with your child.

Don't praise your child's good behavior.

Let your child get away with things because you are afraid of his anger or aggression.

Don't teach your child positive alternatives to negative behavior.

Withhold positive feedback.

Praise only results and not effort.

Don't praise your spouse.

❖ CHAPTER 7 ❖

Teaching Skills to ADHD Children

COMMUNICATION

To teach a child skills or manage a child's behavior, a parent has to practice good communication skills. Communication is even more important with the child who has ADHD. For example, many parents give their child a command to do something when the child is engaged in something else, or even when the parent is not in the same room as the child. Such a command is likely to be ignored, or answered with "in a minute" and then not responded to. The parent typically becomes frustrated and then gets involved in an escalating pattern of reminding the child and then yelling. Other parents will give commands that sound simple enough, but that are really multiple commands embedded in one statement. For example, telling the child to get ready for bed is actually telling him to go upstairs, get into his pajamas, wash his hands and face, brush his teeth, and pick out a book to read together. Parents also directly give the child multiple commands, such as, "Go upstairs, change into your pajamas, and brush your teeth," although when they do this they often find that the first step in the sequence was followed, but the child is now playing with a toy.

How a parent gives commands to a child is important. Parents can use the following checklist as a guide to giving commands effectively:

Were you in the same room as your child?

Did you use a clear and steady voice?

Did you tell your child to look at you?

Did you reinforce eye contact by reminding your child to look at you when his mind started to wander?

Did you give directions one step at a time?

Did you ask your child to repeat the directions to you?

Did you tell your child to let you know when he has finished the first step in the sequence before giving him the second command?

Parents should think about the commands they give to the child. If the commands are actually multiple-step commands, the parents should write them down and see if they can be broken into concrete steps. The example above about getting ready for bed illustrates how this can be done:

Command #1:

Steps for carrying out command #1

Command #2:

Steps for carrying out command #2:

BEHAVIOR MANAGEMENT

Behavior management techniques are important for several reasons: (1) behavior is largely controlled by the consequences that immediately follow the behavior; (2) ADHD children are, more than others, oriented to immediate rather than long-term consequences; (3) these techniques provide structure, consistency, and predictability, which are important for ADHD children; and (4) we have to engineer the environment to provide the rewards or punishments until the ADHD child can provide them for himself.

Many parents feel that the reward systems they set up are too cumbersome or time-consuming, and then failure to follow through consistently becomes a big problem. There are a variety of ways to set up a reward system.

Different Types of Reward Systems

Dividing the Day into Three Time Periods

This method is useful if a parent does not want to keep track of every single occurrence of every behavior. The parent is to pick a problem behavior that occurs frequently throughout the day. This could be something like the child not cooperating, not doing what he is told, fighting with his sister, or using his hands and feet in arguments. The next step is for the parent to identify target behaviors, preferably stating them in a positive way to describe the behaviors the parent would like the child to show, such as: "Cooperate"; "Do what you are told"; "Be nice to your sister"; or "Keep hands and feet to yourself."

Once the behaviors have been identified, the parent can divide the day into three parts. On school days, the first part is the morning, before leaving for school, the second part can be from the time the child gets home from school through dinnertime, and the third part is from the end of dinner until bedtime. On weekends, the first part of the day is from the time the child wakes up until lunch time, the second part is from the end of lunch until the end of dinner, and the third part is from the end of dinner until bedtime.

For each period of the day, the parent can award a sticker or point for the target behavior. There should be a set number of points that have to be earned each day in order to have a privilege, such as television, telephone, or video game time. It is simpler to keep the system limited to a single day, rather than to allow the child to save up points over several days to earn privileges. This guarantees that, in order for the child to enjoy certain privileges on any given day, his behavior has to meet a minimum level of acceptability for that day. Each new day starts from scratch.

A typical chart might look like this:

Target behaviors: Keep hands and feet to yourself
Speak respectfully

	Sun	Mon	Tues	Wed	Thurs	Fri	Sat
Keep hands and feet to self							
Speak respectfully							

Maximum points per day = 6
Rewards:
15 minutes on telephone = 2 points
1/2 hour TV or video game = 2 points

Reward Immediately Following a Specific Behavior

This method is simple and elegant because it involves no chart or stickers. If there is a behavior that is expected at a specific time of day, such as sitting at the table through dinner, it can be required in order to earn a reward that immediately follows that time of day, such as watching television. Another example would be the availability of television, computer, or telephone time only after homework is completed. The child then has a choice as to how long to delay or prolong his homework, possibly cutting into the time available for an activity he prefers.

Many parents make the mistake of allowing the television to go on in the morning when the children wake up. They then struggle to get their children to eat breakfast and dress themselves in time to leave for school. If the television does not get turned on until after the entire morning routine is completed, the children have an incentive to get the routine completed quickly and efficiently, in time to get their reward.

The parents can list behaviors they want to see their child exhibit that can be tied to a specific time of day, such as sitting at the table through dinner or doing his homework cooperatively. Then the parents can list the rewards that can immediately follow those behaviors:

Behavior	Reward

Earning Points for All Privileges

In many situations, it is advisable to put all or most of a child's privileges on a point system. This can be useful when more piecemeal or short-term approaches have not worked, especially when the behavior problem is severe, long-lasting, or pervasive. This is the most extensive and complicated approach to take, and requires the most energy to monitor and maintain. Many oppositional and defiant boys of the preteen or early teenage years respond well to it. This approach gives the parents of these boys a feeling of control. Once the consequences of good and bad behavior are clear and ready to be instituted, the parents find less of a need to yell at the child or get into control struggles. When the consequences of the child's behavior are totally predictable, the consequences become the child's choice. Thus, the parents need not feel guilty for punishing the child, and they can see the consequences as a business-type transaction, where specific behavior results in mutually understood and agreed-upon consequences.

To set up this type of reward system, it is useful to divide the child's privileges into two categories: those that are available on a daily basis, and those that are available less frequently. There may also be privileges that the parents do not want to include in the system, such as a team sport in which the child has a commitment to other members of the team. However, the parents should be careful that they are excluding this activity from the system for a good reason and not just because they are hesitant to make their child unhappy. Daily rewards include telephone privileges, TV, video games, dessert, a later bedtime, snacks, access to toys, and special time with parents. Rewards that are available less frequently are renting a video tape, having a friend over to play, having a friend sleep over, going over to a friend's house, sleeping over at a friend's house, bowling, going out to eat, and going to a movie.

Daily rewards	Longer-term rewards

The point system should include more short-term rewards than long-term. Points can be earned each day and spent as they are earned. Borrowing points that have not yet been earned is not allowed (rewards have to come *after* the desired behavior, not before). Points can be saved—carried over to the following days and weeks. The number of points that have to be spent for rewards has to be in balance with the number of points earned, and it should not be too easy or too difficult to earn privileges. If the child is earning an enormous number of points each week, getting most of what he wants, and saving a lot of points as well, it might be too easy to earn points, and they therefore have little actual value. This situation would be like getting paid more money than one's work is worth. On the other hand, if it is too difficult to earn points and privileges, the child might become frustrated and stop trying.

Once the system is up and running, the point values for good behavior or the number of points that have to be spent for each privilege might need readjusting. The parent should be up front with the child about this possibility from the beginning.

To guide the parents through this procedure, the clinician can instruct them as follows:

> As a first step, list the behaviors that you want to see in your child, for which he can earn points every day. Look at your previous lists in this guidebook to help you, and pick out those behaviors that you can track on a daily basis, such as cooperating with morning routine, cooperating with bedtime routine, sitting at the table throughout dinner, doing homework, cleaning up after oneself, making the bed, clearing the table, keeping hands to oneself, speaking respectfully to others, spending special time with younger sibling, offering to help with household chores, and complying with parents' requests without an argument when asked.
>
> Some of these behaviors can occur only once a day, since they are tied to a specific time or activity, such as the morning routine. Others might occur more often, such as complying with parents' requests. For the behaviors that might occur more than once a day, decide if you are going to award a point for every occurrence, or one point if the behavior was consistently exhibited throughout the day. You might decide, for example, that you make too many requests of your child to keep track of every one of them, or that your child will argue that for every single thing he does, like putting his coat on and taking it off, he should earn a point since he is cooperating. Therefore, having a daily point for compliance might make sense in this case. On the other hand, you might feel that your child never listens, and therefore immediately rewarding any cooperative behavior would be useful. Use your judgment. You can always fine tune the system later.
>
> Now, list the behaviors and their point values:

Behavior	Point value

Before you decide on the number of points your child has to cash in to earn each reward or privilege, estimate how many points he would be earning a day based on his current behavior. Before implementing the point system, without telling your child, keep track of the number of points that you would award him each day for three days, and take the average number of points per day as your baseline.

# of points earned on day 1: ______________

# of points earned on day 2: ______________

# of points earned on day 3: ______________

Average daily points:__________________

It is the goal of the point system to increase the number of points your child earns each day. Therefore, you want to present somewhat of a challenge to your child to improve his behavior in order to maintain the level of privileges he currently enjoys.

With the knowledge of how many points your child would be earning each day, given his current behavior, take his daily and long-term rewards and assign each a point value. Let's say that the average number of points your child would be earning a day is currently 10. Your child should therefore have to earn more than 10 points each day to earn what he likes to do. Remember to include the need to save points for rewards that are not available on a daily basis. Don't make the goals so difficult that your child would not be earning anything. Remember, you can always adjust the point values at a later time. Here's a sample chart:

Points earned

Target behaviors with point values:	Sun	Mon	Tues	Wed	Thurs	Fri	Sat
Total points carried over from previous day							
Total points earned							
Total points spent							
Points to carry over to next day							

Response Cost

Point systems should be, for the most part, reinforcement-based. That is, they should emphasize the earning of positive reinforcers (rewards) for desired behavior. Punishment or negative consequences should be utilized only for behavior that violates major rules, or when positive rewards fail to change the child's behavior adequately.

It is a good idea to start a point system with only rewards and no punishments, if possible. If that does not work, negative consequences can be instituted for undesirable behavior. If, however, the child is already engaging in behavior that is dangerous or otherwise harmful to himself or others, it might be too risky to hold off imposing negative consequences for this behavior.

The term *response cost* refers to the practice of fining the child for undesirable behavior by taking away points. Therefore, his response costs him something. The clinician instructs the parents:

> Just as you had to decide the number of points to be earned for each instance of desirable behavior demonstrated by your child, you now have to identify those behaviors for which your child will be fined and the amount of the fine that you will impose. It is important to impose a fine that will be meaningful, that will have an impact on the child. However, it is also important that the cost not be so severe that he feels it is simply not worth trying anymore because recovery from one mistake will be too difficult. Remember that you can always revise the response costs after you have put the plan into practice if you find that the consequences are too severe or too lenient.
>
> Make a list of the negative behaviors of your child that have not gone away with your positively based point system, or that are so serious that you do not want to wait to see if they go away. Assign a point value between 1 and 3 to each of these behaviors, depending on their severity. A 1-point fine might be imposed for not doing something the first time he is asked to do it, within a reasonable amount of time. A 3-point fine might be used for hitting his sibling. Each instance of these behaviors will be fined

the same amount, so if your child ignores a request to stop doing something a second or third time, he will lose the specified number of points with each refusal.

Negative behaviors	Response cost

To add a response cost to your point system, consider the chart that follows:

Points earned

Target behaviors with point values:	Sun	Mon	Tues	Wed	Thurs	Fri	Sat
Negative behaviors with response cost:							
Total points carried over from previous day							
Total points earned							
Total points spent							
Total response cost							
Points to carry over to next day							

Reinforcing One Behavior for a Long-Term Goal

There might be just one behavior that a parent wants to focus on at present, such as getting into bed on time each night. This type of daily behavior, which is very easy to measure and which occurs a only once each day, is well suited to this method. Have the parent identify the behavior with the child and assign a point for each time the target behavior occurs. Specify a number of points to earn as a goal. When the goal is reached, the child will earn an agreed-upon reward.

Making a grid for a chart might be a good idea, with the number of boxes reflecting the total goal. A checkmark, star, or sticker can be placed in one of the boxes each time the child earns a point. The parent can cut out a picture of the reward for which the child is working and place it at the bottom of the chart. Once the goal is met, the child gets the reward, and the plan can start over. The chart can look like this:

Heather's bedtime reward chart

Place reward picture here.

Setting a Goal to Implement a Reward System

It might help parents to devise an action plan for putting a point system into practice. There are several steps to take in setting up such a plan. The parents can break down the task into its components and set goals for the completion of each step. For example, a parent might want to set up a point system to reward the child for cooperating with his bedtime routine. The goal could be stated as: Set up bedtime point system by Friday, June 5. Then break down the goal into more immediate steps:

1. Decide with spouse on identifying target behaviors and rewards for points by Monday, June 1.
2. Establish number of points needed for a reward and when rewards will be available by Tuesday, June 2.
3. Decide if points will be taken away for noncompliance (response cost) and how many points will be taken. Make a chart listing the target behaviors, their point values, the response cost (if any), and the point values of the rewards available by Wednesday, June 3.
4. Discuss the point system with child, and inform him of your expectations by Thursday, June 4.
5. Implement the system on Friday, June 5.

The action plan can then list all the parents' goals and all the steps leading to those goals in the order in which they will be accomplished:

My action plan

Main goal	Date due	Steps	Date due
Bedtime point system	Friday June 5		
		1. Discuss with spouse, identify target behaviors, and decide on rewards	June 1
		2. Establish number of points needed for reward, and when rewards will be available	June 2
		3. Decide if points will be taken away, and make a chart	June 3
		4. Discuss with child.	June 4
		5. Implement plan at bedtime	June 5

SOCIAL SKILLS

Relationships with peers can be problematic for children with ADHD. They often don't fit in easily, and they feel it. They will butt in when someone else is talking, not wait their turn in games and activities, be loud and aggressive, insist on being in control, become irrationally angry when they don't get their way, not answer when spoken to, not greet others, and ask questions and not wait for the answers. They are often perceived by their peers as being unpopular. They often gravitate to children who themselves are aggressive, hyperactive, or impulsive. They are not invited to friends' homes as much as are other children.

ADHD children often know what to do in social situations. They know they should wait their turn, not interrupt, and share. But they fail to do these things. When asked about their behavior afterward, they might justify it by blaming the problem on others. So, an ADHD child will say he stormed off the basketball court because his friend grabbed the ball. Or he will say that he grabbed the ball because the others wouldn't let him have a turn (the amount of time that he had to wait seemed like an eternity). On the other hand, if ADHD children do things well in a social situation, they might not notice it at all, and therefore they will be less likely to learn from their successes and repeat the positive behavior next time.

Because of the ADHD child's inattentiveness and his lack of an objective perspective on his behavior, he might see what he does totally differently from the way his parents or others see it. He cannot see himself the way others see him. The ability to see oneself greatly helps one's efforts to change.

The Social Skills Report Card is a technique I have found to be effective for parents to use to teach better social skills to their children with ADHD. It also promotes positive, helpful parent–child interaction and a feeling of collaboration in working on the child's problems. The clinician should instruct parents to try to make a habit of observing their child's social interactions regularly. The parents can set up dates for the child to have friends over and arrange to bring her to places where there are other children. If the child is older and more independent, and she is willing to work with the parents on this, they can discreetly observe her when she is with peers.

The parents should communicate to the child that they want to work with her at getting along better with friends. They can identify with the child the social behaviors that they think are important to improve, such as cooperating, taking turns, keeping your voice low, keeping your hands and feet to yourself, letting a friend have his way, making eye contact, saying hello and smiling when appropriate, looking at a friend when she is speaking to you. One or two of these behaviors should be selected to focus on initially. Using index cards or small pieces of paper, the parent can make up two identical "report cards," one for the parent and one for the child. The cards should have the target behavior(s) listed and a blank space for a letter or numerical grade for each. For example:

Take turns

Grade:

Stay calm, and don't argue

Grade:

Immediately after a social interaction ends, or as soon afterward as possible, the parent and child should independently grade the behavior. The parent should use whatever grading system is familiar to the child: A, B, and C; 1, 2, and 3; or Good, Fair, and Needs Improvement. After the parent and the child have written down their grades, they show them to each other and compare them. Then the parent discusses specific behaviors that he observed that led him to give the grade he gave. The child might have given himself an A for taking turns and the parent might have given him a C. The parent then asks the child why he graded himself an A, and he might say, "When Jim wanted to play with a different video game, I let him." The parent might reply, "Yes you did, and that was good. However, I gave you a C because you kept bothering Jim to switch back to the game you wanted to play almost immediately, without giving him much of a chance to play the game that he liked. Do you remember doing that? Jim got so mad he almost left."

On the other hand, the child might have graded himself a C for saying calm and not arguing while the parent gave him a B. When asked why he gave himself a C, the child might say, "I got pretty mad when Jim wanted to stop to get a snack." The parent might reply, "You sure did, but you quickly controlled your temper, agreed to take a break, and you stayed pretty calm the rest of the time."

It is important for the parent to give specific reasons for his grading, and to help the child be specific about his observations of himself because the goal of this exercise is to help the child, over time, to see himself the same way the parent sees him. In other words, he should become more objective about his behavior and better able to judge himself on what he actually did, not on what he intended to do. Over time, the grades the child gives himself should become closer to the grades the parent gives him.

As certain behaviors improve, the parent can use the report card to monitor other behaviors, such as:

Keep hands and feet to yourself

Let your friend be the leader

Say "I'm sorry" when you make a mistake

Say "hello" and make eye contact when you greet your friend

Look at your friend when you speak to him
Ask, don't tell, when you want to change activities
Keep your voice calm and in control
Tell your friend calmly when you are frustrated
Don't grab things
Don't tattle
Walk away when frustrated
Take a break when angry
Share your toys
Ask your friend what he wants to do
Say "please" and "thank you"
Congratulate your friend when he wins
Suggest, don't demand, when you want to do something
Include your younger brother/sister
Ask your friend to stop when he teases you
Tell your friend when you are angry—use words

Parents might use the Social Skills Report Card in several ways: they might focus on one type of behavior at a time in one setting, such as "Keeping your hands to yourself" whenever the child plays outside with peers; they might focus on the child's greeting guests appropriately, whether a peer or an adult; or they might set different social goals in different settings simultaneously.

Lynn was equally concerned about her son Kyle's repeated conflicts with his peers, which arose when he butted in when it was their turn in games, and by the reports from his teacher that he interrupted her when she was speaking to shout out answers, questions, or request permission to go to the bathroom.

Lynn arranged with the teacher to observe her son in school for one hour each week. Knowing that her presence in the classroom would change things for him, she planned to blend into the background as much as possible, rather than taking an active role in volunteering in the class during her observation times. She also thought that by being in the classroom for an hour, Kyle would habituate more to her presence and not notice her as much.

Lynn spoke to Kyle about her plan to observe him, telling him, "I am going to be sitting in the back of your classroom every Tuesday from 11 to 12 in the morning. I want to use the Report Card we talked about to see how your interrupting is going. We will name the behavior we are looking at: 'Waits for teacher to pause before speaking.' Every day that I observe you, we will do the Report Card after school."

Lynn drew up the Report Card this way:

Waits for teacher to pause before speaking
Grade:

For Kyle's peer interactions, Lynn talked to him about his difficulty waiting patiently for his friends to finish their turn when playing games with him. She drew up the following Report Card:

Waits patiently for friend to finish his turn
Grade:

Marla wanted her son Tom to learn how to greet people. She believed that the greeting you give to people is the first and most important single interaction in a social situation because it sets the stage for everything that is to follow during that interaction. If you don't engage someone right away, there isn't much that is going to be accomplished socially after that.

When people came over, Tom would often ignore them. He seldom made eye contact. Marla wanted Tom to develop better eye contact and greeting behavior. She instructed him to make eye contact with family members at home and to greet them verbally. She reinforced and modeled this behavior in her own interactions with Tom. When she felt that he knew what to expect from her cues, she told him she wanted to see how well he did with this behavior when other people came into the home, his friends as well as adults.

Marla developed a report card that she and Tom agreed to use for both his peer interactions and his interactions with adults in the home:

Look person in the eyes	**Say "hello"**
Grade:	Grade:

Marla and Tom agreed that they would each complete this report card each time a guest came into the house but they would wait for the guest to leave before doing so.

ATTRIBUTIONS

When things happen to us, we naturally try to understand what caused them. Not knowing the cause of an event can be so unacceptable that we will make up a cause rather than live without one. Sometimes, this causation-seeking is obvious. If we are in a car accident, we might notice ourselves thinking or telling others: "He came out of nowhere without slowing down"; or "I was in such a rush I didn't look to my right when I entered the road." We don't always do this consciously. However, even when we are unaware of it, we usually make assumptions about what caused an event, and these assumptions influence our feelings and our understanding of events. If we ask ourselves, "Why did that happen?" and think out loud about it, we can often find out what we assume caused something.

There are several assumptions we make about causation that influence how effective we are in the future when dealing with the same problem. A parent might attribute his child's behavior problem to the child's ADHD, placing the cause firmly within the child. Or he might believe he is an ineffective parent, placing the cause within himself. Both of these attributions are to *stable* causes, which means that in the parent's mind, they are not likely to change with time. Attributing the parent's difficulty to his fatigue makes a different assumption than attributing it to his general ineffectiveness as a parent. Momentary fatigue is an example of an *unstable* attribution—one that is not likely to last. So the next time he encounters a problem behavior, he might have more energy to deal with it, making him more effective.

There are other qualities of attributions. For the parent, the attribution to the child's ADHD is an *external* attribution—it is a cause that is outside of the individual making the attribution. Therefore, the parent does not believe that it is his fault. Believing that the problem is caused by his ineffectiveness as a parent is, on the other hand, an *internal* attribution for the parent. Clinicians can guide parents to understand how attributions can impact on our effectiveness in dealing with situations. The following outlines such an approach:

> When we attribute good outcomes to causes inside ourselves (internal), which are also long-lasting and reliable (stable), we tend to feel happy and in control of things. When we encounter similar situations in the future, we tend to believe that we can control them and that it would therefore be worthwhile to make an effort to do so. Such attributions enhance our self-esteem. Or, to look at it another way, people who make internal and stable attributions for good events tend to be people who have good self-esteem.

We tend to feel that we cannot control events in our lives when we make attributions for good things to causes that are external to us and unstable. For example, if we are effective one evening in disciplining our child, and attribute this to our child's being in a good mood, that is an external, unstable cause that does not make us feel good about ourselves and makes us feel less likely to be able to control such events in the future.

For undesirable outcomes, the effects of our attributions work in complementary ways. When we attribute undesirable outcomes to causes inside ourselves that are permanent (internal and stable), such as a belief that we are stupid or incompetent, we tend to feel bad about ourselves and helpless to do anything to change things. The same helplessness occurs when we attribute undesirable things to external, stable causes, such as to our child's neurology, which we believe cannot change. This helplessness fosters a belief that, no matter what we do, we cannot make things better, so we tend to give up trying.

Attributing undesirable outcomes to unstable causes, however, fosters a belief that things can change. If those causes are internal to us, such as a level of skill that can change through learning or practice, we might feel empowered to do something to change our situation in a positive direction. If those causes are external to us, we might not feel so hopeless, as unstable factors change, but we might feel just as helpless, meaning that we still might feel incapable of doing anything ourselves to change things. In other words, we have reason to hope that the situation will change, but there is nothing that we can do to help things along except wait.

In coping with a child with ADHD, the attributions of both the parent and the child are important. For example, if the parent attributes the child's problems solely to his neurology, then she is less likely to take action to help him perform better. She might be willing to consider medication, but she is less likely to be directly involved herself.

If, however, the parent attributes the child's problems to his neurology *and* to the child's skills at coping, *and* to the parent's abilities to understand and manage ADHD, as well as to the parent's ability to help the child improve his own coping skills, the parent is likely to see that there are a number of actions she can take that will improve the situation. That is the premise on which this guidebook is based. With this perspective, the parent is less likely to feel hopeless or helpless.

Children also make attributions, which are important for parents to be aware of. If we do not understand our children's attributions, we might not be able to respond to their successes and failures in ways that will help them. Instead, we will respond to them in ways that are typical and consistent for us, such as with a "just tough it out" philosophy or an "everything will work out for the best" philosophy, whether or not those attitudes are in tune with how our children see the world. In other words, how we respond to our children too often reflects our own attributions and ignores theirs.

Let's consider the situation in which a child fails a math test. Listed below are several different possible attributions that a child might make about this event (even if the child is unaware of thinking these things). Parents should identify whether these attributions are internal or external, and stable or unstable.

Attribution: "I failed the math test because . . ."	**Internal (I) or external (E)**	**Stable (S) or unstable (U)**
I didn't study hard enough		
I'm dumb		
Math is my toughest subject		
The teacher hates me		
I was sick that day		
The teacher grades too hard		
I didn't study the right materials		
I always mess up		
I never do well on tests		
I had bad luck		
My teacher was feeling sick		

Some of these attributions are easy to classify, and some are trickier. The identifications of the above attributions that seem to fit best to me are as follows:

I didn't study hard enough	I	U
I'm dumb	I	S
Math is my toughest subject	I or E	S
The teacher hates me	E	S
I was sick that day	I	U
The teacher grades too hard	E	S
I didn't study the right materials	I	U
I always mess up	I	S
I never do well on tests	I	S
I had bad luck	I	U (unless the child considers himself an unlucky person in general)
My teacher was feeling sick	E	U

The attributions that will most help the child believe he can change the outcome on the next math test are internal and unstable attributions. If the child believes he failed because he did not study the right materials, for example, we can help him think through how to select the right materials for the next test. If the child's attributions are external and stable, it is still possible to help him change them, although it might be more difficult to do so.

For example, consider the attribution "I always mess up." Parents can work with the child to identify what specific behaviors or outcomes make him believe that, and then help him list or identify behaviors or outcomes in which he did not mess up. Once he is able to see that the "always" does not reflect reality, they can help him identify ways to prevent messing up the next time. They might help him to change the attribution "I always mess up" to "I sometimes make mistakes when I don't study hard enough, but if I plan enough time to study I can do well."

If the child believes "math is my toughest subject," he might think this is because there is something inherently difficult about math that won't change, or there is something about math that he is unable to grasp. Either way, this is a stable attribution that the child does not foresee changing. It might be effective, then, and encouraging to the child, to hire a math tutor, or to have one supplied by the school. If the child is open to trying this, it might make math no longer his toughest subject, or it might make him feel capable of mastering his toughest subject. His attribution might change from "math is my toughest subject, so there is nothing I can do about it" (a stable, mostly external attribution), to "math is my toughest subject, so I can find ways to learn it better" (an unstable, predominantly internal attribution). By repeating this latter attribution to the child, pointing out the logic behind it, and having the child repeat it himself, the parents can work on changing the child's attributions.

Parents can now identify problem areas for their child and figure out the attributions that the child probably has for these problems. The child might not be able to tell the parents directly what the attributions are, but they might be able to infer them from what the child says. The parents can write down the child's attributions, as well as whether those attributions are internal (I) or external (E), and stable (S) or unstable (U). Then they can try to find attributions that would be more productive for the child and that have the characteristics that would make the child less helpless or hopeless in facing these situations. They can then work on helping the child change his attributions.

Situation	Current attribution	I/E : S/U	Desired attribution	I/E : S/U

It is equally important to work on the child's attributions for good things. As stated above, attributions for good events are equally important to our feelings of success and failure and to our beliefs that we can do something about these events. Parents can use the same type of chart for deciphering the child's attributions for good events. Let's look at the opposite situation—the child gets an A on a math test. What are some possible attributions, and how are they characterized?

Attribution: "I passed the math test because . . ."	Internal (I) or external (E)	Stable (S) or unstable (U)
I studied hard		
I'm smart		
Math is my best subject		
The teacher likes me		
I just had a good day		
The teacher grades easy		
I studied the right materials		
I do great on everything		
I always do well on tests		
I had good luck		
My teacher was just in a good mood		

This is how I would characterize these attributions:

Attribution: "I passed the math test because . . ."	Internal (I) or external (E)	Stable (S) or unstable (U)
I studied hard	I	U
I'm smart	I	S
Math is my best subject	I or E	S
The teacher likes me	E	S
I just had a good day	E	U
The teacher grades easy	E	S
I studied the right materials	I	U
I do great on everything	I	S
I always do well on tests	I	S
I had good luck	I	U
My teacher was just in a good mood	E	U

The internal attributions for good events are those that would make a child feel better about himself and more in control of things. It might not matter much if the attribution is stable or unstable, as long as it was something the child could control. For example, the attributions "I studied hard" and "I studied the right materials" might be unstable, but if the child believes that one of these factors caused his success, he is more likely to do that the next time. In other words, he knows what he has to do to succeed. If he succeeds like this enough of the time, the attribution will become a more stable one, such as "I really know how to study well."

Now that parents are aware of the attributions that the child makes for good events, they can work at retraining these attributions. The same chart that was used for undesirable events can also be used here:

Situation	Current attribution	I/E : S/U	Desired attribution	I/E : S/U

HOMEWORK

Developing Structure

Homework is a source of nightly control struggles between parents and their ADHD children. This is common for children who are hyperactive as well as for those who are inattentive without being hyperactive. Getting the child to sit and do homework, or even to start his homework, and then getting him to finish it, can take hours of arguing, cajoling, and pleading. Many ADHD children do their homework and then don't hand it in to the teacher because they forget to or they lose it. Therefore, they do their work but don't get credit for it. Some children don't care if they don't get credit for the work they did. One consistent thing that I advocate for children with ADHD is *structure*, both in school and at home. Parents must help provide ADHD children with structure to do their homework, without doing the work for them. If the structure is accepted by the child, his motivation to succeed is increased. By developing this structure, parents can also help the child develop a realistic sense of the amount of time homework takes. Children with ADHD have a poor sense of time. They say they will start their homework "in a minute," but the minute will stretch into an hour. They are also oblivious to the fact that if they start their homework at 9 p.m., they will not finish it by bedtime.

To help the child build his own structure for homework, the parent might sit down with him each day when he comes home from school. After allowing him time to put his books down and have a snack, the parent can ask him to get out his homework assignments. The first step is to have the child make a list of all of the assignments for that day. Then any work he needs to complete that day for any long-term assignment can be added, like a book report or a test he has to study for. Next to each assignment, the child can indicate how difficult he expects it to be. Next, the child can assign a time estimation for how long it will take him to complete each assignment. The child might need help in being realistic in estimating the time, based on his pace of working, the difficulty of the assignment, and his interest in it.

Then the parent can prioritize with the child which assignment to do first, second, and third. The child should be asked, for example, whether he wants to tackle the hardest subject first, so he will have more energy to apply to it, or something quick and easy, to get it out of the way and get some momentum going. It might be a good idea to intersperse difficult or boring assignments with easy or interesting ones. Breaks should be built in, based on the amount of time the parent and the child think he can work productively. A set time for each break can be recorded, and what the child is allowed to do on his breaks should be specified.

One child was successful at developing a very organized chart along these lines, but the plan fell apart as soon as he turned on his computer during his break. Once the computer was on, he got absorbed in whatever game he was playing, and the 5-minute break stretched into a half-hour, causing more discord between him and his parents.

A typical chart, which can be used as a checklist, would look like this:

My homework chart

✓	Priority #	Assignment	Time estimation (including breaks)	# of 3-minute breaks
	1	Math—pages 15–17	6:00–6:25	1
	2	Soc. Stud.—read 28–38	6:25–6:45	1
	3	English—write 1-page essay	6:45–7:30	2
	4	Health—find magazine article on cholesterol	7:30–7:45	

Breaks will be every 15 minutes for 3 minutes. During breaks, I will be able to:

1. Get a drink or snack
2. Talk to someone
3. Lie down
4. Watch football on TV

Initially, the parent will probably need to provide a good deal of the structure for the child, and model good organizational behavior. This help can be gradually phased out as the child takes over more of the responsibility for this system. For example, when the parent first sits down to plan with the child, the parent can introduce the ideas of listing the assignments, estimating the time it will take to complete them, and prioritizing the order in which to do them, based on the child's interest and the level of difficulty of the subject areas. The parent can act as the child's scribe, recording the information in the chart. The child and parent should discuss what to do and not to do during the breaks, and how often to take the breaks; whether or not to use a timer; and, if not, how the child will keep track of the time.

The next day, the parent should go through this process again, but this time having the child write the information on the chart. Then the following day, the parent can have the child estimate the time needed to complete each assignment, with the parent helping him judge whether he is being realistic. On the day after that, the child can do the time estimations and list the assignments in order of priority. The child takes over one more aspect of this process each day until he is doing it with minimal cuing from the parent.

Since children with ADHD often complete their work very slowly, it might help to monitor how much work the child can produce in a given period of time and try to improve it. For example, if 15-minute work periods have been set up, as above, the parent can record the number of math assignments that were completed in this period of time, or the number of pages of a report that were written, or the number of language arts worksheets completed. The parent can then set a goal with the child to complete slightly more work in the next 15-minute period, and then record that. The child might enjoy making a game of this without it getting frustrating.

Amount of work completed in initial ______ minute period:

Goal for amount of work to be completed in 2nd _____ minute period:

Amount of work completed in 2nd _____ minute period:

Goal for 3rd ______ minute period:

Amount of work completed in 3rd ______ minute period:

THE HOMEWORK SETTING

Where a child does homework is often the source of much conflict and debate in the home. Many children do their work at the kitchen table, in the room in which most family life takes place. Many parents prefer this arrangement because they are there to monitor the child while they perform other duties, like preparing dinner. The disadvantage is that there are many distractions and interruptions for the child. Siblings run in and out, the television can be heard from the other room, the parent is helping the siblings with their homework, which is interfering with the child's concentration, and the phone is ringing. However, when I point this out to parents, many are still reluctant to have their child with ADHD do her homework in her room. They have observed that when she goes to her room and sits at her desk alone, she gets nothing done. Her mind wanders, she looks at her toys, and she doodles. She seems to need the presence of others to stay on task.

Other parents get into struggles with their children as to whether to allow them to do their homework in front of the TV or with the radio on. They have been instructed to minimize distractions for their child, and the TV and radio are incompatible with this idea. The child often insists that he gets his work done better with the TV or radio on. The reality is that some children with ADHD do get their work done more efficiently with more stimulation surrounding them and some do not. It is well accepted that children with ADHD need stimulation in order to attract their attention. They attend better when there is novelty and a high stimulus value to their tasks. This can mean, for some, that increasing the stimulation of the setting in which they are working can increase their attention to task. Working in a quiet, unstimulating environment can increase their boredom and make their minds wander. On the other hand, many children with ADHD tend to be highly distractible. Stimuli other than what should be the focus of their attention can pull their minds away from their tasks.

We do not know enough about how the nervous system of children with ADHD works to know why some do better with environmental stimulation and some do not. But, just as the most effective medication dosage can be very specific to the individual, the balance of stimulation in the environment seems to be idiosyncratic as well. So, when a child with ADHD tells her parents that she studies better with the TV or radio on, she might be right or she might not. But this is something the parents can study more objectively. Without telling the child that they are monitoring her productivity, the parents can record the amount of time that it takes the child to do her homework, and how much homework gets done, with the TV or radio on or off. Although it is impossible to control for the same amount of homework every night, keeping track of this for two weeks should give the parents a good idea of the situation in which their child works most efficiently.

The parents can develop a chart like this:

Day	TV/radio on ✓	TV/radio off ✓	# of assignments	Amount of time

The parents should make sure there is a balance in the number of days that they allow or disallow the TV or radio during homework. Once this monitoring is completed, the parents can present the chart to the child and discuss the issue more objectively.

Children and adolescents with ADHD often feel they were doing better at getting their homework done and handing it in, but when their grades come out they fail one or more subjects because of the number of missing assignments, which they were totally unaware of. It is clear that paying attention to homework is not these children's strong suit, and, like a lot of things in their lives, they could use help in becoming better at monitoring themselves. This would also help the parent to keep them on track when they start to derail.

It would also help the parents to keep track of the child's daily school performance if the parents are basing the child's access to specific privileges on completing the schoolwork. Since typically there are several weeks between progress reports or report cards, it is hard to base short-term rewards, like daily access to the car for a teenager, on school performance.

In elementary school, a school counselor can work with the child to collect a daily report from the teacher on what assignments and homework have been completed, the child's behavior in school, and any test scores from that day. In middle and high school, the student can be responsible for bringing the following chart to his teachers each period, and for bringing it home completed each day.

Date	% of work completed	Homework done?	Behavior	Test grades	Teacher signature
English	100 75 50 25 0	Y N	Cooperative Uncooperative		
Math	100 75 50 25 0	Y N	Cooperative Uncooperative		
Social Studies	100 75 50 25 0	Y N	Cooperative Uncooperative		
Science	100 75 50 25 0	Y N	Cooperative Uncooperative		
Language	100 75 50 25 0	Y N	Cooperative Uncooperative		
Health	100 75 50 25 0	Y N	Cooperative Uncooperative		

With this chart, the parent doesn't have to wait to reward the child for getting good grades. The parent can track the behaviors that go with good grades on a daily basis. Minimal standards can be set, based on this chart, that the child has to maintain in order to earn certain privileges on a daily basis, like using the telephone, or on a less frequent basis, such as going to a school dance. For a longer-term goal like the latter, the parent can establish the number of days the standards must be met in order for the child to go to the dance. To guard against the child's earning the required number of points and then returning to noncompliant behavior the day before the dance, the parents should require that the child also conform to expectations during the two days prior to the dance.

SEQUENCING SKILLS

The ADHD child's poor sense of the passage of time, his variable attention to details, and his impulsivity make recalling events in their proper sequence difficult. Sequencing information is an important cognitive ability for understanding cause and effect, using feedback from the environment to help one plan and act more effectively, and learning to take responsibility for one's own actions. Sequencing is important in learning how to cope with transitions, anticipating and preparing for change, and developing better social skills.

For example, a child might feel justified in hitting another child who called him a name. In reporting on the event, he might omit important details, such as the fact that he grabbed the other child's paper out of his hand in the classroom earlier in the day, or that he pushed the child the day before. If the child does not recall the events that led up to the incident accurately, in their sequential order, he will not see his own responsibility for the problem. If the child reports an incident in which he got into trouble or in which he participated, and he externalizes blame, helping him to sequence the events that led up to the incident might help him see his role more objectively.

The parent can suggest going over the incident step by step, writing down the events as the child recalls them, while leaving spaces between events to be filled in later as other events are recalled. The parent can begin with the most immediate events and with what the child clearly remembers, and then calmly question the child as to what happened immediately before and after the events that were recalled. The parent can expand the list to include anything that transpired between the involved parties on the previous day or days.

Once the list is completed with the events in their proper sequence, the parent can review the sequence step by step with the child, pointing out each party's responsibility for his actions, and also pointing out moments when a different decision or choice on the part of the child might have altered the eventual outcome.

When Emma was home with her two children, for example, and trying to get things done around the house, she was often interrupted by screams coming from the family room, followed by her 10-year-old son Michael running up to her complaining, "Joseph hit me!" After repeated questioning, Joseph would admit to hitting Michael, but it became clear that Joseph's aggression was the end of the sequence of actions between the two boys, rather than the beginning. Although Michael was the one who complained to his mother, he was also the one who usually set in motion the sequence of actions that led to his complaints.

The next time this happened, Emma sat down with Michael and Joseph with a marker and paper, and asked them to tell her everything that happened. She wrote down each event, attempting to get the sequence right, and leaving blank spaces where she thought she might have to add information.

Eventually, her list looked like this:

> Michael asked Joseph if he could use Joseph's action figure.
> Joseph said no.
> Michael pleaded with Joseph and argued with him.
> Michael took Joseph's action figure.
> Joseph screamed and tried to grab it back.
> Michael pulled away and pushed Joseph away from him.
> Joseph hit Michael.
> Michael screamed and complained to mother.

Another sequencing problem that often occurs with children with ADHD is that of starting their day and getting off to school in the morning. Many parents allow this time to be more chaotic than it has to be by not adhering to the same sequence of behaviors each morning. The parent can post a schedule of behaviors that are expected, in sequence, and put copies of them in prominent places in the house, such as on the child's mirror and on his door. For the older child, time expectations could be added to each behavior. For the younger child who cannot read, magazine pictures can be cut out and pasted to the chart, illustrating each step in the sequence.

DEVELOPING EMPATHY IN THE CHILD

Parents can tell a child that being bossy or lying is wrong, and he might be able to say that he shouldn't do those things "because they're wrong."

However, if he is 8 or younger, he might not be able to say why they are wrong. Helping a child to understand the consequences of these types of behaviors can cement his acceptance of the idea that he should not act that way. With the young child it is necessary to be both very concrete and to approach it in a step-by-step manner.

If a child has been told not to be bossy, it is important to help him talk about what this means. The child should be asked what he was doing that was bossy in specific detail. Then, with the parents using these behaviors or similar ones as examples, the child should be asked to imagine someone being bossy to him. For example, if the child was bossy when playing with his friends, the parent could talk to him about how he grabbed the ball from one friend and demanded that other friends stand in certain positions during a game of catch. Later, he got angry when some of his friends wanted to change the order in which the ball got tossed between them.

Once these behaviors are established, the parent can ask the child how he would feel if they were playing catch and he wanted to throw the ball, but the parent grabbed the ball out of his hand before he could do it, and then the parent insisted that the child stand in a certain spot that he didn't want to stand in. Once the child understands how he would feel, he can be asked how he thinks his friends feel when he does that to them. If he can acknowledge how his friends feel, he can then be asked why he thinks bossiness is a bad idea. The parent can go beyond the fact that it makes people feel bad to other consequences, such as it makes kids not want to play with him and it makes kids angry at him. The parent can extend that into a discussion of why these outcomes are undesirable to the child, such as not wanting to lose friends or have people mad at him.

The parent then needs to discuss alternative behaviors with the child. For example, if the child wants to do something a certain way, the parent can work with him on asking his friends rather than telling them what to do. If his friends say no, the parent can work with him on accepting this or on suggesting that he and his friends take turns deciding how to do things. One should always include the potential positive and negative consequences of each decision.

To provide a constant reminder and reference point for the child, the parent might want to chart these discussions so he can keep a visual record of the topics that were discussed. When these problems come up again in the future (and they will), the parent can get out the chart and go over it again. If new problems crop up, the parent can see if the solutions that were worked out previously for other problems can provide some guidance as to how to talk about and handle the new ones. The parent can keep a notebook of these charts.

A chart can look like this:

Topic	Behaviors	How I would feel	Consequences	Alternatives	Consequences
Being bossy	Grabbing, giving orders, not listening	Mad, sad, hurt	Kids won't want to play with me, kids won't have a good time, kids won't want to be my friend, friends will be mad at me, friends won't come over to play	Asking instead of telling, letting others have their way, asking to switch off how we do things, putting up with being bored instead of complaining	Friends will have a better time, more kids will like me, kids will want to play with me, kids won't be mad at me, friends will let me have my own way more

USING EVERYDAY ACTIVITIES TO DEVELOP SKILLS

A parent can teach a child a lot of practical skills by introducing them into everyday activities that the parent and child share. Here are a few ideas:

Playing Games

Playing a game with a child is a good opportunity to coach her on taking turns and following rules. If the child starts to change the rules or cheat when she is losing, or when something bad happens to her in the game, the parent can point out the behavior and its possible consequences. The parent can say, "When you get frustrated, you change the rules," or "When you get frustrated, you stop following the rules." The parent can add, "Do you think other kids will like it if you do that? How do think they will feel? Do you think that they will want to play with you again? How would you feel if you were winning and another kid did that?"

If a child is following the rules, tolerating frustration, and waiting her turn, the parent can give her frequent verbal praise, such as, "You're doing a great job waiting your turn," or "That must be frustrating, but you're handling it like a good sport." This provides an opportunity for the parent and the child to work on impulsivity. The parent can ask the child if she knows what a "good sport" is, and discuss good sportsmanship and its relationship to making and keeping friends.

Games also offer good opportunities to work on sequencing skills. After the parent's turn, for example, he can ask the child: "What will happen next?" If there is a decision point for the parent, such as buying a property in Monopoly, he can ask, "What do you think I'll do? Will that be better or worse for me? How? Will that be better or worse for you? How?" If it is a decision point for the child, the parent can ask her to pause before making the decision and ask, "If you do this, what will happen? If you do this other thing, what will happen?"

If the child has to do something about which she has no choice, such as sliding down a chute in Chutes and Ladders, the parent can ask her how she thinks that will affect the game (who will be winning?), how it would be possible for her to catch up, and whether one of you can remember if someone caught up from behind earlier in the game.

When the child gets frustrated in a game, or experiences a setback, the parent can explore her attributions and help her develop alternative ones. If she does slide down the big chute in Chutes and Ladders, and says in an annoyed tone of voice that she is going to lose the game, the parent can talk to her about how saying that actually makes her more upset, and explore the times that someone was behind and caught up. The parent can point out to her the value of saying, "I'm behind, and I can still catch up like I did before," or "I'm behind but no one knows who will win," or "I'm behind, so I have to try harder and not give up." If the child wins the game, the parent can point out how her original thoughts would have led her to quit, and if she had done that she never would have experienced winning. If she continues the game and loses, the parent can praise her for playing fairly and not giving up.

Eating Dinner

Having dinner as a family can be an important teaching opportunity in many ways. Manners can be taught and reinforced. Children can experience the benefits of asking for things politely and of being treated politely by others. Impulsive actions, such as reaching too quickly or not looking, can have immediate, unpleasant consequences, such as spilling things, soiling clothing, or hurting people by dropping hot food on them. Impulsive children can be cued as they sit down to a meal to think before they act and to pay attention to where their body is and how fast it is going. They can be praised for waiting for something to be passed to them or for looking before grabbing or passing something themselves.

Sequencing skills can also be reinforced at dinner. Since you can't eat everything at once, the child can be taught to accept, for example, that dessert comes after the main course has been finished and the table has been cleared. Dinnertime is also a good opportunity to reinforce the child for not interrupting in conversation. Each occurrence of this behavior should be immediately followed with praise.

The Parent's Talking on the Phone

The parent's talking on the phone can be problematic for children with ADHD and their parents. The child needs to be taught to wait without interrupting, to keep the noise level down, and to find alternative ways to amuse himself if what he is doing is not compatible with an adult talking on the phone. To further these aims, the parent can sit down with the child and discuss the behaviors that are desired when Mom or Dad gets a phone call. The parent can point out examples of interrupting, waiting patiently, making too much noise, playing quietly, and finding something else to do. The parent can then ask the child what he thinks would be good ideas of things to do during the phone call so as not to interrupt. Once acceptable behaviors are agreed upon, the parent can make a list of these behaviors and post them near the telephone. The parent can point to this list when he is on the phone if the child needs a reminder. The parent can also work out other cues to signal the child to quiet down (a finger to the lips for example), wait to speak (showing the palm and fingers raised), or find another activity (pointing with the index finger or rolling one's hands around each other in circles). Whenever the child responds appropriately, the parent should praise him lavishly when he gets off the phone. He can also review with the child what the child did that was good, much as he would do when going over the Social Skills Report Card.

Transitions

Everyday life provides parents with plenty of opportunities to teach children how to cope with transitions. With the ADHD child, it is important to break down each transition into short steps and train the child to progress through the sequence with less supervision over time. Although transitions present some of the same issues as do other daily events, such as playing games and eating dinner, there are some skills that are unique to them. One such skill is anticipation of the immediate future. Children with ADHD are notoriously poor at anticipating. They often have a poor sense of the passage of time, and are deficient in the ability to project themselves into the future. Although they might experience the same routine or sequences of expectations repeatedly, they fail to develop a sense that each part of the routine is predictably followed by another part, as parts of a larger whole. So, when the child is playing with a friend close to dinnertime, he might be so absorbed in the moment that he neglects to consider that playtime must end soon, and he must put away his toys, say good-bye to his friend, and walk him to the door. Or, in the morning, the child might get so absorbed in breakfast that he neglects to leave enough time to get dressed without rushing.

Cuing the child about a pending transition is helpful: "It's close to dinnertime, so it's time to clean up your toys and get ready to say good-bye to Sam"; or "It's time to be finishing your breakfast so you have enough time to get dressed." To help the child become better at cuing himself, after the parent has served as the cue for a few times he can then preface his reminder with: "I am going to give you the same reminder I always give you . . . " After a few of these, the parent can then start asking the child, "What is the reminder that I usually give you at this time?" thereby prompting the child to cue himself. The cues can get briefer over time. After doing this, the parent can cue the child at the beginning of the activity: "Try to remind yourself when it's time to clean up, say good-bye, and get ready for dinner." The parent should offer abundant praise when the child cues himself.

Some situations can be particularly challenging to the ADHD child's ability to cope with transitions, such as the child coming home from school, one or both parents coming home before dinnertime, getting ready for school in the morning, the evening bedtime routine, and transferring between the homes of divorced or separated parents. It might help to develop a written script or a sequence of events for these situations, and to review them prior to each transition. For example, if a divorced father is preparing his child to return to the mother's home at the end of the weekend the father can make a chart that looks like this:

Transition to Mom's house	
3:30	Finish homework.
4:00–4:15	Get books and clothes ready and put on jacket. Prepare to leave.
4:15	Get into car with Dad.
4:15–4:45	Drive to Mom's.
4:45	Enter Mom's house. Say hello. Put coat and backpack away.

Each time this transition occurs, the father can get out the list, read it aloud, and have his child read it aloud as well.

Another example is transitioning to the child's soccer game:

Transition to Soccer	
8:00	Turn off TV and put away toys.
8:15	Get water bottle; make sure it is filled.
8:20	Put on shin guards and cleats.
8:30	Put on sweatshirt, if needed.
8:35	Be ready to get into the car.

The parents should make similar charts for all transition times.

PRIORITIZING TEACHING GOALS

From among these skills—taking turns, following rules, coping with transitions, sequencing, handling frustration—the parent can identify those with which the child needs the most help, the situations that are the most opportune for teaching these skills or in which these skills are most needed, and the parent's goals as to when he will work on these skills with the child:

Skill	Priority #	Teaching situations	Date and time
Taking turns			
Following rules			
Transitions			
Sequencing			
Frustration			

ORGANIZATION

Children with ADHD often do not remember where they put things. They lose their homework, important announcements from school, and so forth.

Physical Belongings

The knapsacks of children with ADHD are like black holes where everything goes in and nothing comes out. These children need help to get organized, and their parents need to be actively involved in the effort. It is not enough to teach children how to organize their papers and knapsacks; it is essential to train them to practice these skills when they need to. For example, if parents ask a child where his homework papers for each subject belong, he knows which folders are for which subjects, and that he is to put his homework papers in the folders immediately upon completion of the assignment. If parents ask him how he should clean out his knapsack, he knows he should throw away any outdated notices, and file class notes in his notebooks and graded papers in a file at home. He might even know that he should do this once each week. However, getting him to *do* this once each week is another story, and involves practice and monitoring.

Parents can begin by setting up a schedule for one of these activities and a plan to *shape* the child's behavior. *Shaping* behavior means developing a behavior that one wants in a child by rewarding behaviors that gradually come closer to the target behavior until the goal is reached. The behaviors that are rewarded progressively approximate the behavior that one desires. Parents should start with a behavior that the child finds easy to do and after he has mastered it, the parents should teach him to do the next step, which will involve taking on more responsibility, thereby coming closer to the goal.

Organizing homework papers needs to be done every day that the child is assigned homework. Organizing the knapsack is something that can be done once a day or once a week, depending on how serious the problem is. The parents start with a weekly knapsack check. Plan with the child a specific time each week that the knapsack will be checked. A good time might be Friday before or after dinner, or some other time on the weekend. Or, if weekends are too hectic, some other time near the end of the week might be good, such as Thursday after school. Post the day and time in a prominent place, or places, such as on the refrigerator and on the child's mirror or door. At the first planning session with the child, the parents should engage his help in developing a list of the steps to go through to complete the procedure. Write down all the essential steps and then make sure they are in the correct sequence. A sample list for a knapsack review is as follows:

Frank's knapsack review

#1 Set the timer.

#2 Empty the contents of the knapsack onto the kitchen table.

#3 Sort the contents into the following piles: (a) trash, (b) class notes, (c) papers to be filed, (d) papers to give to parents, (e) papers to bring back to teacher, (f) other

#4 (a) Throw out the trash. (b) Put the class notes in the appropriate notebooks. (c) File papers to be filed. (d) Give parents their papers. (e) Put papers to return to school in the front of the knapsack. (f) Do what is needed with the remaining papers.

#5 Write down how long this took you. Try to complete this task faster next time, or if you are satisfied with your pace, make it the same next time.

Organizing a child's homework is a daily task, at least on weekdays. It is a good idea for the parent to set a time that this will be scheduled each day. There might be some variability depending on the day of the week, after-school commitments, and the parent's work schedule. A sample list for reviewing homework organization is as follows:

Frank's homework organization chart: to do after each assignment

#1 Put completed assignment on desk.

#2 Take out homework folder for that subject. Place homework into the folder.

#3 Place folder into prearranged place in knapsack.

#4 When the last assignment is completed, check that all assignments are in the correct folders and that the folders are in the correct places in the knapsack.

This project should be begun by the parents' leading and coaching the child through each step. Once this is going smoothly, on a subsequent day, the child can complete the first step by himself, and then be coached through the following steps. The child can sequentially take over one additional step at a time, until he is doing the entire sequence by himself.

VERBAL MEDIATION AND RULES

Children with ADHD often have difficulty remembering rules and sequences of behavior that are expected of them. For example, parents often find themselves repeatedly reminding their children about each step in their morning or evening routines, as if they have never gone over it before. Children also seem to forget the basic behaviors that are involved in meeting people or making friends, and seem to be doing it for the first time, no matter how many times they have struggled with it. Many parents find themselves repeating things several times with their children, or telling the child to repeat back to them what they have just been told. *Verbal mediation* is a way of helping the child to provide this guidance for himself, by training him to talk to himself as he is performing a task.

When working with a child to organize his homework every day, as we discussed above, and he is at the point of performing several steps on his own with little or no guidance from the parent, he can assist himself by repeating the steps to himself in a low voice as he does each part of the process. The child is therefore trained to talk his way through the process. With enough repetitions this script becomes part of him. It becomes more automatic. This technique can be applied to social skills as well. If a new child has moved into the neighborhood, and a parent wants his ADHD child to begin a possible friendship with the new child on a positive note, the parent can arrange an introduction and coach his child on a proper sequence of behaviors when he meets his peer. The parent can prepare him for the meeting by helping him figure out the words that he would be comfortable saying. He can outline the sequence of behaviors like this:

1. Say, “Hello, I’m Adam.”
2. Smile.
3. Ask him what he likes to play.

The child can repeat this sequence to himself in a low voice, in preparation for saying it to himself silently when he meets his friend. It should be made clear that this is a technique to help him if he needs it, and that he need not remember to do it exactly this way when he meets the child. We don’t want the child to freeze if the sequence is disrupted by his forgetting or by something unexpected happening, such as the peer being very friendly and having a lot to say, making the rehearsed sequence irrelevant.

The parent can think about situations in which training the child in verbal mediation might be helpful. This technique can be applied to a wide range of situations, such as homework, mastering math problems, social skills, and self-care. It is especially applicable to tasks that involve sequences of behaviors that have a limited number of steps. The parent might write down two situations in which he wants to attempt this method. Then the parent can write down the sequence of behaviors in each situation. The parent should remember to keep the descriptions of each behavior in the sequence brief and to the point.

A PARENT’S ABSENCES

It is more difficult for the child with ADHD to spend days apart from a parent than it is for most children. The situations in which this might happen include when a parent travels, and when parents are divorced or separated and the child has to spend days with one parent away from the other. With the noncustodial parent, this situation is a part of daily life. With the custodial parent, it occurs when the child is visiting the other parent for a weekend or for an extended period of time.

It is therefore important to give the child concrete ways to keep the absent parent in mind. One obvious way is for the absent parent to call every day. This might not always be practical and it might not be sufficient. The parent should plan to provide the child with visual reminders. Pictures of the parent are useful. It might also be helpful to provide the child with a written itinerary as to where a traveling parent will be on each day of her absence. For example, the parent can work on filling in a calendar with her location written on each day, as well as indicating in large letters when she is scheduled to return home.

For a noncustodial parent, it might help to have a calendar on which to record the activities that the parent and child will do together during a visit. If the parent formulates these plans when he is not with the child, he can write them down and mail, fax, or e-mail them to the child. It might also be helpful to provide the child with information about the parent's daily schedule and daily life, to help the child envision the parent as a human being who has an existence between visits. Making a recording of the parent's voice is another possibility for reinforcing the child's relationship with an absent parent. The recording can contain a message for the child to play each day, and can range from a simple "Good morning" to good luck wishes for a special event that day, to a reminder about important rules that the child is expected to follow. Leaving a child a note to find every day is another possibility. The notes can also remind the child of activities that the parent will engage in with the child when the parent returns, such as going out to breakfast, taking a trip, or going to the beach. Parents can write down what types of visual or auditory reminders they want to provide their child with, and the dates by which they intend to put them into effect.

SELF-SOOTHING

There are various methods that can be used to teach a child to calm himself. What works depends on the child and the situation. Children with ADHD can be quite volatile. They overreact emotionally to events and have a hard time turning off their emotions once they start.

Examples of methods that can help a child calm down:

1. Getting face to face with the child and coaching him in a quiet voice to calm down.
2. Putting one's hands on the child's shoulders and quietly telling him to calm down.
3. Coaching the child to close his eyes and count to 10.
4. Coaching the child to take several deep breaths.
5. Holding the child firmly but gently.
6. Quietly sending the child to his room to calm down before any further discussion takes place.
7. Using words to label the child's behavior, such as "fussy," "busy," or "too much," so the child will recognize these states in herself and associate this with the need to calm down (after being coached by her parents).

The parents should think of the situations in which their child overreacts emotionally and loses control. When does this happen? What methods work for the child in these situations? The parents should write them down and use them to try to help the child soothe herself. It is important that the parents calm themselves down before they can be helpful to their child.

Situation	Soothing Method

Now the parents can select one of these situations to work with. They can pick a situation in which the child consistently has difficulty calming herself and choose a method that they will try with the child in this situation. The parents can record what they did and how it worked. Then they can try it again. They can assess if they were more effective the second time. They can then evaluate whether or not they want to try the same method a third time, alter the method, or try a different approach. This process is useful because often parents get into the rut of doing the same thing that doesn't work time after time. This is especially true in emotionally charged situations, in which parents get "hooked" and lose rationality and perspective.

Situation	Calming method	Did it work? (Y/N)	Did 2nd attempt work? (Y/N)	Try again, modify, or change? How?	Did it work? (Y/N)

Using the same table, the parents can select other situations and work on their calming methods with their child.

AGGRESSION

Hyperactive boys are especially prone to aggressive behavior. The mixture of impulsivity, poorly regulated emotions, and poorly controlled activity makes them vulnerable to reacting aggressively to frustration rather than considering alternatives. Parents also give their children mixed messages about aggression. We tell our children to "walk away," or to "fight back," or to "walk away first and fight back if you have to." Often mothers and fathers give their child different messages about aggression, confusing the child. Fathers might take pride in their sons' aggression and might vocally support it. Or they might verbally tell their child not to fight, but nonverbally communicate that it is okay to do so. Mothers often have a more detailed knowledge of their child's peer relationships. They might know the peers with whom their child is more likely to end up fighting, which peers are more likely to pick on their child, which peers their child might need to defend himself against, and which peers can be dealt with best by ignoring and walking away.

It is important to give clear messages to the child about aggression, and about how the parents' thoughts apply to the different peer relationships the child has. The parents can then help their child understand which peers to avoid, which to tell on, which to joke around with physically, and which to defend himself against if necessary. A parent can also help the child recognize the signs of anger building up in himself, such as his face feeling warm, his teeth clenching, his heart beating faster, and his voice getting louder. Parents can list the messages they want to give their child about aggression and tie them to specific, practical peer situations. It would be most helpful for both parents to work on this together in order to give their child consistent messages. They should be aware of the biases that they have that are gender related. A father might have a greater tolerance for, and even an encouragement of, aggression, while a mother might have an absolute intolerance of it. As stated above, mothers might also have a greater knowledge of the child's social relationships. So, it helps if the parents are open-minded and try to see that their biases might be influenced by their sex or their prior experiences. These factors should be respected, but they can also interfere with objectivity.

Situation	Appropriate response

Parents can also teach their children the consequences of aggression. Aggressive behavior is a good example of the compelling nature of impulsive actions as well as the pull of short-term results over long-term consequences. Parents can brainstorm with their aggressive child about what feels good about aggression and what the long-term outcome might be.

Jill and Tim reviewed this issue with their daughter Tiffany, and Tiffany came up with the following good points about hitting her sister:

1. It feels good.
2. It stops her from bothering me.
3. It gets me my way.

After discussing this problem, Tiffany was also able to acknowledge the following disadvantages to hitting her sister:

1. My sister won't like me as much.
2. My sister might hit me back.
3. My sister won't want to play with me.
4. My sister won't want to share her toys with me.
5. Mom and Dad will be disappointed in me.
6. I won't learn to use my words to get what I want.

To help Tiffany, Jill and Tim first had to agree that it was unacceptable to them that Tiffany hit her sister for any reason.

PARENTS' OWN THOUGHTS AND FEELINGS

Children with ADHD know the pain and frustration that comes from other people expecting the worst of them. Children who are predominantly inattentive often find that their teachers think of them as lazy or unmotivated. Their parents often expect them not to do as well as they are capable of doing in school. Hyperactive and impulsive children are often the first ones blamed when something bad happens. These children often tell me that they are the ones who get singled out when two or more children are talking in class or horsing around.

Parents might have expectations or beliefs about their children that they are not even aware of. These might influence how they interact with their children, thus affecting the children's self-esteem. For example, most children dawdle to some extent at bedtime. This is also the time of day when parents are most likely to feel tired and depleted. They have worked all day, at their jobs or at taking care of the children and the home, and they just want some peace and quiet. With the child who is expected to give the parents a hard time, any minor annoyance is likely to trigger that "here we go again" feeling in the parents. When they have gotten to the point where they have this expectation of the child, there is little difference in how they react to minor or major annoyances. Even normal hassles in the routine become catastrophized. Their emotional reaction communicates to the child that he is a royal pain even when he is doing what most children normally do.

If an ADHD child is fighting with a sibling or friend, the parents might rush into the room with these thoughts just outside of conscious awareness: “He’s always starting fights,” or “He can’t get along with anyone for more than five minutes.” They might assume that the problem was caused by the “problem child” and blame him or punish him more quickly than they would the other child. Parents’ thoughts and beliefs about the child influence their feelings about him and how they interpret events in which he is involved. Although these thoughts are probably based on many actual negative experiences with the child, they also set up the parents to expect the worst and to interact negatively with him more of the time. These thoughts make it more likely that the parents will react more punitively to the child than they would to another child for the same behavior, and less likely that they will recognize and enjoy the child’s positive behaviors. The child will also come to expect more negative reactions from his parents, and will have difficulty seeing them as a source of positive reinforcement.

It is important, therefore, for parents to examine their own beliefs and assumptions about their child, so they can correct any tendency they have to blame or find fault more than is realistic or helpful. As a first step, the parents should consider the time of day when they feel that their child’s behavior is at its worst. If it is bedtime, then the parents start the evening expecting things to go wrong, waiting for something bad to happen, and ready to pounce at the slightest provocation. If there is another child who happens to be generally well behaved, the parents might notice that when this child does something to disrupt the evening routine, they are better able to tolerate it and have a sense of humor about it.

The parents should think about times when they expect trouble from their child. It might be the bedtime routine, as mentioned above, or the morning routine. Or the parents might dread it when the child comes home from school every day, anticipating another suspension, detention, or bad conduct report. The parents should write down the two or three worst times of the day or week, and what their thoughts and feelings are just before this time of day:

Time of day	My thoughts and feelings

The parents should reflect on how these thoughts and feelings cause them to react or overreact to their child's behavior:

My thoughts and feelings	My reactions

Then the parents should think about how they would react to a child of whom they had positive expectations. They can write down how they would like to change their reaction to their child during these times, perhaps having more patience, or waiting to react until they have all the information, or listening for positive information, or reacting to negative behavior firmly but not punitively:

Time of day	How I would like to react

Before the next time they typically expect something negative to happen, the parents can review their notes and coach themselves to react differently. Spouses can coach each other on following through with their goals. Parents can choose one of these times to start with and set a goal as to when they will plan to react differently and how:

Situation	Date and time I will change my reaction	What I will do differently

A WAY TO PUT THE CHILD IN CHARGE

I have developed a technique that puts the child in charge of changing his behavior and avoids any implication of blame toward either the child or the parents. It also helps to circumvent control struggles over the child's behavior. I have found this technique to be highly effective with children of all ages with all types of behavior problems. This technique can be adapted by parents to use at home.

The first step is to define the problem to the child in behavioral terms that are free of blame, criticism, or judgment. The parents must be neutral in terms of whom they are holding responsible for the problem. For example, if the parents want to address the constant fighting that goes on at home between them and their child, they can say to the child, "There are too many fights. We don't know how they start or why they keep happening. We want you to do something important for us over the next week. We would like you to keep track of the number of fights or arguments that we have by marking them down on a chart." The child is asked to keep track of the number of fights and arguments on a daily basis, and to decrease the number of fights so that each day the total is lower than the previous day's total.

The child might protest that he does not start the fights, or that his parents are blaming him, or that he should not have to change because his parents are unreasonable, or that unless his parents are willing to change, he should not have to. The parents can reassure their child that they are not blaming him for the fights or letting themselves off the hook. The parents should agree that all of them have to do things differently. They should not get into specific details about the fights they have. They should tell the child that they value his perspective and that he can be a great help to the family by doing this. The child is then asked to record each fight or argument by marking an X in the lower section of the chart on the appropriate day. Each subsequent argument will be marked by an additional X above the previous one, making a graph of the number of fights the child is involved in each day. The child is reminded that on each day, the goal is to have fewer fights than the day before. If the number of fights exceeds the number from the previous day, the child should be told not to worry, just to continue with the goal of having fewer the next day.

The parents should not tell their child specifically what he has to do to decrease the number of fights, just to do it. He will find a way to do it more easily if he doesn't feel he is being blamed for it. This way, he is free to attribute the cause of the fights or their improvement to whatever works for him, and to whatever makes it possible for him to stop the behavior. So, if it works for the child to see himself as making life better by arguing less, or by not engaging his parents when they are being unreasonable, he is free to believe whatever makes it possible for him to behave differently.

When the attempt to decrease fighting is successful, the parents should give their child a great deal of praise for providing a useful service to the family. Although the child will not be blamed for the fights, he will receive credit for decreasing their frequency, and the parents can point out to him how much better his life is now that he is not spending so much time arguing with them. Keeping track of the number of incidents of fighting or any other problem behavior also teaches the child self-monitoring skills. Children with ADHD are often unaware of how often their behavior is a problem to others. At the end of each week, the parents should review the chart with their child. If the child has been successful at decreasing the number of fights, he should be given a great deal of praise for the valuable contribution he has made to the family.

The chart should look like this:

	Sun	Mon	Tues	Wed	Thurs	Fri	Sat
10							
9							
8							
7							
6							
5							
4							
3							
2							
1							

This chart can also be used for monitoring other behaviors:

Not listening to parents
Teasing his sister/brother
Yelling and screaming
Talking out in class
Not doing homework
Fighting with friends

When the child presents the chart at the next family session, he might proudly show the therapist how well he did, or he might sheepishly say that things did not go too well and show the therapist a day or two in which there were many negative behaviors. It is important for the therapist and the parents to praise the child generously for every day in which there were few or no negative behaviors. Each day in which the child was successful in this way is an important event. The therapist (or the parent at home) should count the number of days in which this success occurred and announce the total in an enthusiastic manner to the child. Then make another chart for the coming week and encourage the child to do even better.

Although this chart was developed as an attempt to eliminate negative behaviors, there is no reason not to use it to try to increase positive behaviors in children through self-monitoring. Children could be instructed to keep track of the frequency of the following behaviors, and advised to increase the number of occurrences each day:

Cooperative statements to parents (such as, "Yes, I will do that")
Positive interactions with siblings
Kind and gentle interactions with parents
Homework periods that end with good feelings
Play periods with peers that go well
Sharing with siblings
Listening to parents
Doing homework
Doing chores
Walking away from arguments and fights

❖ CHAPTER 8 ❖

Working as a Parenting Team

If parents are honest with themselves, they realize there are some situations that they handle well and others that they don't handle well. They might find themselves dealing calmly with getting the kids off to school in the morning but losing their temper during the bedtime routine. Or they might find themselves regularly becoming irritated with the children about their behavior during dinner. Repeatedly getting into struggles with their child is not good for the parents or the child. If this happens on a regular basis, it might signal that there is something about the way the parents cope that needs attention.

Maybe the parents are more fatigued and have less patience at the end of the day. Maybe they are in a rush and therefore have less patience at the beginning of the day when they have to get off to work or get the kids ready on time for the school bus. Perhaps the child's poor behavior at the dinner table is especially annoying because of the way one or the other parent was brought up. The parents might be bringing something to the situation that makes discipline more difficult. If this is the case, it would be helpful for the parents to recognize the situations that are difficult for them and, if possible, the reasons why. Then they can figure out if they can change the situation or let their spouse take over in order to decrease the level of stress in the family.

The parents can divide the day into its component parts and activities, as in the chart below. They can then add items to the day that are part of family life. They can assess how skilled each parent is in handling each of these situations.

Activity/time of day	**Mother** **1 = Usually effective** **2 = Usually ineffective**	**Father** **1 = Usually effective** **2 = Usually ineffective**
Morning routine		
Midday activities		
Dinner		
After dinner		
Evening routine		
Bedtime		

The parents can then look at the times in which they are usually ineffective. What is it about those times or activities that makes them less effective than at other times? For example, are they more tired or rushed at those times of day? Are they trying to do too many things and therefore cannot concentrate well on any one thing? Are they attending to the child but actually trying to get to something else? Do certain things make them angry, such as poor behvior at the dinner table, or children refusing to clean up their toys? Writing these down might help the parents get a better perspective:

Activities when I am ineffective	What makes me ineffective

Now they can add another column to this list: "What Can I Do About It?" Possible solutions are letting the spouse take over dealing with the children in those situation, changing one's expectations, changing the demands on the parents so that they have more time or energy to focus on the situation, and using humor to change the parents' interaction with their children.

EXAMPLES OF POSSIBLE SOLUTIONS

Letting the Spouse Take Over

Between 5 and 6 PM every day, Marie had a hard time preparing dinner and keeping her two children safe and happy. It was what she referred to as the "witching hour," in which her children were a combination of overly tired and wound up. They were more likely to get into fights and to overreact emotionally. She was constantly "putting out fires" while she tried to work in the kitchen.

As her work schedule was more flexible than her husband Tom's, she was home earlier and, rather than rest herself, she got dinner started. Part of the way through this chaos, Tom came home. He would briefly greet everyone, and then go upstairs to change his clothes and wash up. Then he would come downstairs and look through the mail as he talked to Marie.

Marie and Tom had become so accustomed to this routine that they did not consider that they could do it any other way. In counseling, they discovered that they had more flexibility than they realized. Marie asked Tom if he could leave work fifteen minutes earlier, either by shortening his lunch hour or by saving certain phone calls or paperwork until the next day. Tom was able to do that on most days. When Tom came home, he agreed to interact immediately with the children and take over managing their behavior, rather than going upstairs and then looking at the mail. Once dinner was ready to be served, Tom would supervise seating the children at the table and then go upstairs and quickly change his clothes.

Having Tom take over minding the children at this time of day greatly relieved Marie's stress and eliminated a source of unspoken resentment between Marie and Tom and Marie and the children.

Changing One's Expectations

Paul was very strict at dinnertime, insisting on near-perfect table manners, and intolerant of his daughter's slow pace of eating. He remembered dinnertime in his parents' house as a chaotic affair in which everyone talked at once and bickered with each other. Sampling food from each other's plates was a common practice. Paul wanted dinners at his house to be relaxed, orderly affairs. However, his insistence on order was so exact that mealtimes were hardly relaxed.

Recognizing the personal issues that he was bringing to the table, Paul was able to relax his expectations and let his daughter be a child.

He let her squirm in her chair more, sing songs, and act silly. He was able to ignore some of the minor instances of her eating with her hands. He was also able to allow her to linger over dinner after he and his wife had finished, and permit himself or his wife to get on with other things while one stayed longer at the table with their daughter.

Changing the Demands on the Parents

Frank came home from the office every day in time to spend a good part of the evening playing with and talking to his children. He even arrived home in time for dinner many nights. However, he always brought home a lot of unfinished paperwork, and he had to make telephone calls to clients.

Frank was fairly relaxed through dinner and after dinner, and thoroughly enjoyed his children. When it came to their bedtime, however, he became more anxious, as each minute of procrastination or delay on the part of his two children made him worry about having enough time to complete his work demands so he could get to sleep at a reasonable hour. Frank found himself rushing the children at bedtime and having little tolerance for their playfulness. He saw their silliness as oppositional, and rather than working with them, he strictly demanded that they follow their routine without deviating from it.

Almost every night was stressful for Frank and his children, and this for a father who usually enjoyed his children and went out of his way to spend time with them. Frank recognized that he was putting a lot of pressure on himself during this time of day, which translated into pressuring his children, who really were not doing anything unusual. He had led himself and others to expect that he would be available by phone in the evenings and that his paperwork would never be delayed.

Frank decided to spend an extra half-hour at work at the end of the day when he had phone calls to return. He would also make more of an effort to return phone calls, and at least leave messages for the people he could not reach, during his lunch hour and in the few moments he had between meetings. He was able to feel good enough about this reasonable effort to reach people to carve out the evening as his family time. He also gave himself permission to extend the time in which he expected himself to complete nonemergency paperwork, and told himself that people would understand and tolerate it as long as his work was of good quality.

With a lot of the pressure off in the evenings, Frank was much more tolerant of his children and enjoyed the evening routine much more. Remarkably, much of the children's behavior problem cleared up.

Using Humor

Julie's daughter Michaela liked to be in control. Getting Michaela washed, her teeth brushed, and into her pajamas at night was a struggle, as Michaela was constantly diverted by more interesting things to pay attention to, like her image in the mirror. Seeing her reflection in the mirror was, for Michaela, an invitation to make silly faces and act out dialogues in funny voices. When Julie tried to supervise Michaela's evening routine, Michaela would order her mother out of her room, and try to force the door closed. This usually led to a control struggle, with Julie becoming more angry and strict about enforcing her rules, and with the atmosphere becoming an unhappy one.

One day, when Michaela closed her door on Julie, Julie politely knocked, and said, in a mock British accent, "Excuse me, m'lady, if you please, I would like to deliver some tea and scones to you to assist you in the completion of your nighttime responsibilities." After some initial resistance, Michaela became more playful and engaged in the game with her mother. Julie was able to play-act with Michaela in this way through most of the rest of the evening routine, thereby being on hand to supervise and direct, and maintaining a positive atmosphere with Julie in charge.

STEPS THE PARENTS CAN TAKE

Now the parents can add the third column to the previous chart and see how many ways they can think of to change things.

Activities/times when I am ineffective	What makes me ineffective	What I could do differently

Now the parents should have a better sense of the times that they feel ineffective, and what contributes to their feeling that way. They should have a sense of what they could change to make themselves more effective, and at what times their spouse might be able to take over and be more effective than they are. The parents can arrange a time to sit down with each other to prioritize these changes and to set a date on which they will implement them.

We will make the following changes on the following dates:

1)	DATE
2)	DATE
3)	DATE
4)	DATE

Division of Labor

By recognizing what one's spouse does well and what one does not do well, a parent might decide that it is not worth trying to change him- or herself, and that it would simply be best for the parent and the spouse to do what each does best, and stop trying to master every situation. So, if one parent is more patient with the evening routine and the other has not been able to muster the energy to deal with it calmly, the more patient parent can take over. In return, the other parent might take over getting the children ready for dinner every night. It's best for each parent to be honest with what he or she can and cannot change, and to work out a mutually beneficial division of labor with each other.

There may also be times when both parents believe they can handle the same situation adequately, but they disagree on methods. One example that I use in *Fathering the ADHD Child: A Book for Fathers, Mothers, and Professionals* (Jacobs 1998) concerned two parents who had different definitions of what behavior indicated that their son had eaten an adequate amount at dinner. One parent defined "eating what is on your plate" as meaning that literally every morsel of food that was put on the child's plate had to be eaten. The other parent defined the term as meaning that the child at least had to try some of each type of food that was on his plate. As the parents could not agree on this point, they agreed to switch off nights when each was in charge of the rules at dinner. They informed their son as to which parent's rules were in place for the evening ("Tonight we are using [Daddy's] [Mommy's] rules for dinner"), and the child adapted to this. So, alternating who's the boss is often a viable alternative.

The Parental Tag Team

A parent decides to handle a situation but gets in over his head. He's more tired than he had realized and the child gets to him more than he had expected. The parent is becoming so frustrated that he loses his temper. The parent can do what professional wrestlers do in tag team wrestling—have his partner take over and get out of the ring! There is no shame in getting out of a deteriorating situation. In fact, it is nobler than ending up being a screaming idiot and red in the face because one's 5-year-old got the better of him. Of course, the agreement to do this has to be worked out between the parents ahead of time rather than in the heat of battle.

Seeing oneself as part of a tag team also means that there is nothing wrong with asking for help when one needs it. It is better to recognize when we are not doing something well than trying to tough it out and compounding our mistakes. It's not just one's ego on the line, it's one's relationship with one's children!

Learning Empathy

Maybe a parent is told by his spouse that he doesn't understand his children. He might be told this because of repeated instances of the child breaking down in tears when the parent tries to get her to do something, or because the parent always ends up yelling at the child. Instead of taking this as criticism, the parent might want to take it as helpful, realistic input. If a parent doesn't understand his children, it is best not to fight it, but to learn from it!

Empathy is the ability to experience the feelings of another person. It is more than just sympathy, where we express concern or support for another person's feelings. It is the ability actually to experience what the other person is experiencing internally, to see the world through his or her eyes. To empathize with another person, we have to draw on our own experiences with the same feeling and suspend our preconceived ideas of what the other person is feeling or should be feeling. This is not the same as drawing on our experiences with the same situation. If a child is distressed because she has lost a toy, it is not enough to imagine how we would feel if we lost something, because losing something might not have the same meaning to us as it does to the child. We would have to draw on the distress we would feel in a situation that would be emotionally similar to us, that would cause us the same degree of distress or confusion. For us, that might be something like forgetting to bring a report to an important business meeting.

To develop empathy, we have to be able to observe other people without first imposing our own needs and perspectives on them. Parents might want to set aside fifteen to twenty minutes one day to observe their child without commenting on his behavior or interacting with him. This could be when the child is playing or when he is interacting with others. The parents should observe the child to learn about his interests and emotional reactions without trying to change or direct him. This can be especially difficult for many fathers to do. After the parents have been able to do that, they should interact with the child in a way that follows his lead. If he is playing with toys, for example, they might make a few comments that remark on what he is doing, limiting them to the child's behavior: "The soldier is going into the fort," or "The baby is crying." They should not impose their own ideas, assumptions, or directions onto the activity, but try to see the world from the child's perspective rather than from their own.

Empathy can help parents in several ways. It helps them understand how far to push their child to do something before he gets too frustrated. What is easy for them might be too difficult for the child. Knowing the child's limis will help parents avoid many control struggles. Empathy helps parents know what punishments will be meaningful to their child, rather than imposing something that does not bother the child at all or that bothers him too much for him to see the point. Empathy also helps parents avoid humiliating their child. Often, when we react out of our own anger and frustration, we say or do things that are destructive to the child's self-esteem. A long-term pattern of doing this can have a permanently detrimental effect on a child's self-esteem and confidence. If we are empathic to our children, we will be able to understand their experience of the situation, rather than seeing only our own frustration. Empathy also helps parents understand their spouse's limits—what is too frustrating for her, how her mood might affect what she is capable of in any given day, and when she might need your help.

Putting Emotions on the Back Burner

Parents might be endowed with an overabundance of empathy, but that can also get in their way. If they empathize too much, they might be disarmed from following through on things that they ought to follow through on because they are afraid it would upset the child. Parents might need help in putting their emotions on the back burner in order to set limits in a businesslike way.

Parents can solicit feedback from their spouse when they have trouble separating themselves from the child's emotional reaction. Maybe they feel sorry for the child when she gets upset at having privileges taken away from her. Maybe the parents delay setting limits for too long because they don't want to be the "bad" parent. Maybe they try so hard to understand the child that this derails them from taking action when appropriate. Whichever parent is better at being "businesslike" in setting limits can "train" the other parent in putting his or her emotions aside when necessary and in distinguishing between what is true distress in their child and what is manipulation.

It might be a good idea to identify those emotional reactions in the child that give each parent trouble, as well as how these emotional reactions get in the way. For example:

Emotional reaction in child	What it makes it difficult for me to do
Crying	Taking away privileges
Anger	Enforcing Time Out

Now that the parents have identified their problem areas, they can solicit help from one another. They can ask for feedback on how to enforce limits in the face of their feelings of guilt or anger, or whatever reaction disarms them. They can help each other differentiate between what is true distress in their child and what is learned behavior. They can sort out what feelings they are assuming their child has because of their own experiences or their own childhoods, and how that might be different from what their child is actually experiencing.

OFFERING HELP, GIVING FEEDBACK

For parents to work together, they must be able to talk to each other. They also have to know how to listen to each other. It is not good enough to tell a spouse that he or she is doing something wrong. How they say it determines if it is truly heard and whether it changes anything.

The general tenor of the parents' relationship is vitally important. If there is an air of anger and distrust, simply changing the language they use to communicate criticism won't help much. If one parent experiences the other as too critical, defensive, argumentative, or angry, there is a serious lack of trust that must be dealt with first. If problems can be talked about, there is a much better chance of resolving them. Parents might need to have some discussions about how each perceives the other and what they hear when they talk to each other about the children. If they can resolve to try to listen to each other, talk to each other respectfully, and put aside their assumptions about the other, they can begin to work at communicating more effectively.

Another thing parents should keep in mind is that how they think they are saying something might be very different from the way it is heard. One parent might insist that he is being kind and helpful while his spouse might tell him he is being insulting. Provided each parent is making a good-faith effort to communicate well, it is important to help a parent understand what it is about his or her communication that the spouse finds insulting and to help the parent respect the fact that, to the spouse, the experience of hearing him or her in that way is insulting, whether or not that is what the parent intended or that is what the parent would feel in the same situation.

Too many couples get into too many struggles about what really happened rather than focusing on what their experiences are. Experiences are the reality we are dealing with. So, the argument—"I did not insult you!" "Yes you did!"—is pointless. Insult is in the eyes of the beholder, and if the parents respect each other and their relationship, they will not want the other to feel insulted.

One woman was frustrated by her husband's inconsistencies in following through with what he promised. She found his replies of "I don't mean to hurt your feelings" even more frustrating and dismissive. She told him, "I know you don't mean it. If I thought you were the type of person who was capable of intentionally hurting my feelings, I wouldn't have married you. But you *do* hurt my feelings and we have to change this."

Once parents have committed themselves to listening to each other and talking to each other in positive ways, they can agree to give each other honest feedback about things that each of them feels need to change, and they do so with respect, collaboration, and diplomacy.

I try to help the parents realize that if their spouse is having a hard time with their child, they must be feeling pretty bad about it. If one is going to criticize someone's behavior, it is good to empathize with how she might be feeling. It is important first to address one's spouse's frustration, anger, sadness, or feelings of inadequacy. If one's spouse feels understood, and that his or her feelings are being validated, then the spouse will be more open to feedback.

IMPROVING A PARENT'S LISTENING SKILLS

Parents often feel so emotional about their children's behavior that they argue with their spouses rather than listen to them. They also feel that their spouses do not listen to them. Not listening and not feeling listened to usually occur together in the context of a relationship for which both people share responsibility. If a person can improve his ability to listen to his spouse, the chances are good that his spouse will be better able and more willing to listen to him.

Many times I have heard one parent say to the other, "You're not listening to me," only to have the other parent respond, "But I *am* listening!" Being listened to is also in the mind of the beholder. One might feel that one is listening, but what counts is whether the other person feels listened to. In the heat of emotion in dealing with their children's problem behaviors, parents often cut each other off, insisting that their point of view be heard and giving little credence to the other person's perspective. They discover that they are capable of acting just as impulsively as their children!

It might help a parent to solicit feedback from his spouse or from another adult about how he can improve his listening behavior. The feedback should be phrased in positive rather than negative ways. For example, rather than being accused of interrupting all the time, it would be better to hear: "Practice patience. Wait for the other person to finish before stating your point of view." Telling someone to stop doing something does not tell the person what to do instead. It is more helpful for a person to hear what the other would like him to do. It is also better for one's self-esteem to have a project or goal that will lead to improvement than to be criticized for something.

Parents should think of what feedback to give to their spouse in a positive way. They might find it helpful to write down what they want to do better and what they would like their spouse to do better:

What I can do better:

1)

2)

3)

What my spouse can do better:

1)

2)

3)

The parents can choose a time to review these plans with each other, a time when they both can talk and they are not dealing with the children. They can make an agreement to give and listen to feedback on these points the next time they are discussing the children's behavior.

RESPECTING DIFFERENCES

There will be rewards and punishments that one parent thinks make sense, but that make the other parent feel uncomfortable. Rather than getting frustrated with one's spouse, it is more helpful for the parent to try to understand why these are objectionable to her, and respond to these feelings whether he thinks they are rational or irrational. After responding to one's spouse's concerns, she might still be uncomfortable. Rather than trying to force one's opinion upon one's spouse, it is important that the parent respect his spouse's discomfort and try to find another solution to the problem. There is always more than one way to respond to a child's behavior. If either parent is uncomfortable with a plan, it is going to be difficult to carry it out fully and wholeheartedly, which means that the plan will be weakened or undermined.

One parent might think, for example, that it would be a great idea to give her child small amounts of money, like an allowance, for every day that he cooperates. Her spouse, on the other hand, might be uncomfortable using money for a reward in this way. There might not be a reason for this objection that makes sense to the objecting parent, but if something feels uncomfortable, there might not be a way to get around it, and it just has to be respected. So, a great solution is only great if both parents are comfortable with it and are committed to working it out and seeing it through.

For every "great" idea that has been rejected by one parent, the parents should try to generate two or three alternatives that are worth trying, and discuss them. The parents can add to the list of alternatives, then narrow them down to the most appealing ones, and select one to start with.

"Great" ideas	Alternative solutions	Alternatives worth considering	Solution to start with
A)	1)		
	2)		
	3)		
B)	1)		
	2)		
	3)		

DELAYING DECISIONS ON CHILDREN'S REQUESTS

Children often make requests as if they are life-or-death matters that must be decided NOW. Children are naturally impulsive, and children with ADHD can be more impulsive than most. Parents often feel pressured to agree to something on the spot, later realizing that they are not comfortable with what they agreed to, and fearing that there will be hell to pay if they change their minds. I try to tell parents of ADHD children, who are often impulsive themselves, that it is perfectly all right to tell their children that they will get back to them with an answer later, or that they need time to think about the request or to talk to the other parent. The power to make decisions also includes the power not to make them, or to put off making them, and it is all right to expect the child to adapt to that fact of life.

To deal with their own impulsivity, parents can think of decisions that they have felt pressured into by their children, and then visualize themselves responding to their children's insistent requests with a delaying statement. They can then write down several of these delaying statements and practice them in their mind, so they will have them ready the next time they need them:

Delaying statements

PRAISING ONE'S SPOUSE

Just as many parents have difficulty praising their child nearly as often as they criticize him, many couples have a praise deficit in their relationship as well. Spouses become very good at telling each other what they do wrong, especially in families under stress. It becomes easy for parents to overlook, forget about, or take for granted all of the good things the other parent does. Spouses take each other for granted. The many daily things they do for each other often get lost in the background. It is the crises and the annoyances to which they end up attending and responding.

Parents who are under the chronic stress of raising a child with ADHD often have to be trained to praise each other, just as they have to be trained to praise their child. Parents can make a list of all of the things that their spouse does for them or the child, as well as the things they do that contribute positively to their well-being and the well-being of the family, such as exercising or eating well. They can then check off how often they give verbal praise to their spouse for each of these activities. A sample chart can look like this:

Activity	Number of verbal praises per week
Use behavior management techniques effectively	
Praise our child	
Stay calm dealing with behavior challenges	
Walk away from control struggles with child	
Play with child	
Take time to exercise	
Stay out of parental control struggles	
Help child complete homework calmly and efficiently	
Help child calm down	
Prepare dinner	
Run errands for the family	

After a week of monitoring his or her praise behavior, each parent can then try to increase the number of verbal reinforcers that he or she uses in each category for the next week.

GETTING THE CHILD OFF TO SCHOOL

One problem that comes up repeatedly is the child who constantly has difficulty getting ready on time in the morning for school. Parents must keep reminding, pestering, cajoling, and yelling at the child. When this happens, the parents must be coached through a careful sequencing of the morning routine, with an "ace in the hole" in case all else fails, which I will describe later.

Often, after parents complain about their child's noncompliance with the morning routine, they add that they just can't get their child to turn off the TV and eat breakfast. But what is the TV doing on before breakfast? So many parents have grown accustomed to their children turning on the TV in the morning that they don't even question whether it should be on. The basic principle that highly desired activities should be used as reinforcers for less desirable activities only works when the highly desired activity (watching TV) follows the completion of the less desirable activity (eating breakfast or getting dressed). If the child is already watching TV, he is getting the reward without meeting his responsibilities. So, the first issue is that the TV should not be on until all of the child's other responsibilities have been met. Then, the quicker the child meets his responsibilities, the more time he will have to watch TV. The more time a child takes in completing the morning routine, the less time he will have to watch TV. The child will experience how his behavior directly determines what he can and cannot enjoy. With that established, the parent can be helpful in making it clear to the child what he must accomplish in order to have time for TV in the morning. Writing down the sequence of activities that have to be completed, and having it visible for the parent and child to refer to in the morning, makes these responsibilities clear-cut.

The parents can make a list on posterboard, illustrated with pictures, or tape a list to the child's mirror or dresser. The list should include getting dressed; washing; eating breakfast; brushing teeth; getting books, book bags, homework, school supplies, lunch and other essentials ready and in their proper places to be brought to school; getting outerwear ready; and whatever else the parents deem to be essential before the child walks out the door.

Now, the "ace in the hole" I mentioned earlier is very useful in eliminating all the pestering, reminding, and nagging that goes on in the morning. After setting up clear expectations in this way, the parents can then tell the child: "The school bus (or the car) leaves at exactly 8:10. You will be on (in) it in whatever state of readiness you are in. If you are not completely dressed, I will put you on the bus (in the car) in your underwear/pajamas/socks and put the rest of your clothes in your backpack. I will call the school and tell them that you were not dressed in time to leave for school, and since we feel that being on time for school is so important, you will be arriving at school with the rest of your clothes in your knapsack and could you please finish getting dressed in the principal's office."

Parents should be warned that this should only be done if they are absolutely sure that they will follow through with it. Children can tell when their parents are bluffing and they will gladly call their bluff, giving them even more power. If the parent is driving the child to school, the car has to leave at exactly the designated time and no later.

I have seen many parents take this approach, with children of all ages, and I have never seen it fail. I have only had one report of it being tested, and once the parent followed through it was never tested again.

❖ CHAPTER 9 ❖

Cooperative Parenting after Separation or Divorce

Separation or divorce is one of the most disruptive and emotionally troubling experiences that children go through. The typical adjustments that children and their parents have to make to separation and divorce are intensified with a child who has ADHD. The child with ADHD might have trouble keeping in mind the activities that he was anticipating doing with the noncustodial parent during the week, and might have great difficulty adjusting to the different rules and ways of doing things in his parents' two households.

It is vitally important that the noncustodial parent remain involved and present in the child's life, not just on weekends or during visitations, but on a daily or near-daily basis. Ongoing contact with both parents is crucial, even though having frequent contact with two parents who disagree and who have different homes and different rules might exacerbate some confusion and behavior problems for the ADHD child. The loss of a parent can have profoundly detrimental long-term effects on a child's self-esteem, ability to form healthy relationships, and ability to behave in socially acceptable ways.

KEEPING A MENTAL IMAGE OF THE NONCUSTODIAL PARENT

It is important for the child with ADHD to have some tools to keep the image of the absent parent in mind. Since these children often have difficulty anticipating the future, reuniting with a parent who has not been there can be more jarring than it is for a child without ADHD.

The following tools might help:

- The noncustodial parent can give the child several pictures of himself, or himself with the child, to carry around with her, to pin up in her room, and to keep in her school bag or other places.
- The noncustodial parent can make a calendar with his child and circle when they will see each other again, and write down what they will do. Then the child can look at the calendar and remember. The calendar should be colorful and stimulating, with photographs and drawings.
- The noncustodial parent can call every day, if only to say "Good night" or "Have a great day!"
- The noncustodial parent can send a tape recorded "letter" or e-mail frequently, to which the child can respond.

DIFFERENT RULES AND LIMITS/TRANSITIONS

Children with ADHD typically have a difficult time transitioning from one setting to another. Two divorced parents might have different ways of doing things, and might disagree, but it is important that each understands the rules in the other home and helps the child adjust to them.

It might help for the parents to list the different rules and expectations that exist in the two homes. They can include the differences in schedules, table manners, behavioral expectations, chores, and responsibilities. These should be all the things that the child has to transition to and might need help with.

Rules and Expectations	
Dad's house	Mom's house
1.	1.
2.	2.
3.	3.
4.	4.
5.	5.

To help my child with each of these transitions I will explain to her:

ACCOMMODATING TO THE EX-SPOUSE'S NEEDS

Noncustodial parents often see the concerns of the custodial parent as being overblown and unrealistic. After all, when they are with the child, he is generally well behaved and, when he challenges authority, he is easy to bring back under control. It is important for the noncustodial parent to understand that the custodial parent has a different experience of the child that is valid for him or her.

Usually, children behave worse for the parent who spends more time with them. Because the noncustodial parent doesn't see the undesirable behavior doesn't mean it doesn't happen, and it doesn't mean that the custodial parent is incompetent because of the problems she experiences with the child.

It is important for the noncustodial parent to take seriously the difficulties the custodial parent has with the child's behavior, and to be as supportive as possible for her attempts to set limits and deal with the problems productively. Not believing the custodial parent, or considering her incompetent because of these problems, usually gets communicated in some manner to the child, and thereby serves to undermine the custodial parent's authority.

While the custodial parent might not have the right to control what the noncustodial parent does during his time with the child, she might make some requests that could be reasonable, given the child's ADHD. For example, the custodial parent might find that her son is returned to her Sunday night "all wound up" from his active weekend with his father, and is especially hard to settle down because he has fallen asleep in the car on the way home. She might request that the father try to give their son a nap earlier in the day, and try to prevent him from falling asleep in the car. It is in the child's interest that he be able to settle down at night, control his behavior, and go to bed without difficulty. The noncustodial parent might see this as an attempt to control him and his time with the child, or he might try to see if he can accommodate this request in some way.

The noncustodial parent can think of the requests that are made of him by his ex-spouse that indicate that she has a different perception of the child's problem behaviors. The noncustodial parent can consider which requests might be valid even if he doesn't share that perspective or observe the problems to the extent that his ex-spouse describes them.

The noncustodial parent can write down these requests, while putting aside his own animosity toward his ex-spouse, and thinking of how he might be able to accommodate them for the sake of his child:

Request 1:

Request 2:

PUTTING THE CHILD IN THE MIDDLE

Unfortunately, divorce or separation is often accompanied by a great deal of animosity between the parents. There are often feelings of betrayal, profound disappointment, and anger at the spouse and at oneself. There are troubling feelings of guilt and failure. These feelings can make dealing with one's ex-spouse very painful.

Children link parents to each other for life. Parenting not only forces parents to have contact with each other and to rely on cooperation, but also serves as a constant reminder of the other parent, even in times of no direct contact.

Many people, often unwittingly, lean on their children for emotional support or confirmation of their thoughts and feelings about the other parent. They might say negative things about the other parent to the child, or they might say negative things to others, in person or on the telephone, when the child is in the house and able to overhear them. Some parents might say little or nothing directly, but their bitterness will somehow be communicated to the child.

Another way children are put in the middle between their parents occurs when the parents tell the child too much about their disputes, such as details of their financial arrangements or court proceedings. Some parents leave important court documents out on the kitchen table where the child can sneak a peek at them if he wants to. These actions place the child in a very unhealthy position. Out of loyalty to one parent, she might feel compelled to adopt his beliefs and take on his anger. This only alienates her from her other parent, causing grave psychological damage. The child needs both parents and should not feel forced to choose one or the other in terms of love and affection.

This is an opportunity for the parents to think honestly about the things that one parent does or says that puts the child in the middle of the conflict between himself and the other parent. The parent should consider what he says to the child, what he complains about, how he makes his ex-spouse's life difficult when it comes to arrangements for the child, and the resentments that he has that might be expressed indirectly to the child. The parent can get some feedback from someone he knows. He can write down what he hears. The parent can then resolve not to do these things. He can say to himself what he will do, in a positive way, for example: "I will discuss my problems with my ex-spouse only when my daughter is not at home or with me," or "I will keep all papers and correspondence concerning my disputes with my ex-spouse in a private place where no one else can see them, at all times." The parent can write down these resolutions as concrete reminders to himself, which he can refer to in the future

CONFUSION ABOUT AUTHORITY

One issue that comes up repeatedly in my practice is the confusion over authority that the ADHD child experiences when his parents separate or divorce. I find that this confusion is often greatly exacerbated, unwittingly, by the actions of the parents.

Family therapists cite the importance of the integrity of the parenting subsystem, or the parenting team, in the maintenance of the structure of the family. Dysfunction follows the breakdown in communication and teamwork among the parents, and the formation of cross-generational alliances, in which one parent and a child become more strongly allied with each other than the parents are with one another.

Even when the parents are split up, they must maintain some alliance for child-rearing purposes. Of course, in separation and divorce, the integrity of the parenting team is disrupted. Communication, too, is disrupted and is often hostile, nonexistent, or counterproductive to raising children in a healthy manner.

A common issue of disagreement between two parents who could not stay married is child rearing. The parents' differences in styles might be much more obvious if there is no longer a pretense of being a parenting team after they divorce. One or both parents might become more vocal about differences.

Children with ADHD often escalate their problem behaviors—their noncompliance, challenges to authority, or violations of important rules and expectations—when their parents split up. In this situation of divided authority, it becomes more difficult for the child with ADHD to keep the rules and expectations straight. Understanding that certain behaviors are expected in one home but not expected in the other home is more confusing for the child with ADHD. There might be increased testing and challenging of authority by the child with ADHD, as there could be for any child in this situation. Each parent must be steadfast in maintaining the role of a firm and consistent authority figure.

Complicating and often undermining these efforts to maintain parental authority in these situations is the introduction of another adult into the life of the child. Divorced or separated parents who choose to live with a new partner often complain that the child challenges the authority and gets into vicious control struggles with the new partner. Why, the parent wonders, does the child not respect the authority of the parent or of the live-in partner? Further complicating this situation is the outrage that the other parent often feels that the live-in partner is trying to discipline his or her child. In this situation, the authority of the parent who is cohabitating is threatened. Introducing a new adult authority figure into the life of a child with ADHD whose parents have split up is complicated enough. When that person is a live-in partner, rather than a married spouse to the parent, the potential problems are compounded.

A parent who remarries is introducing a new parental figure as a stepparent. This person has a certain legal standing in the household. Not only is there legitimacy for this person's role as a parent, but because the parent and stepparent have chosen marriage, the stepparent has at least made a commitment to the parent and the child. This commitment provides some rights and privileges, both legally and psychologically.

The role of a nonparental adult in the household is much more ambiguous. A nonparental adult, even if he or she is determined to take a hands-off approach to the child, has to assume the role of authority figure sometimes and in some ways. This is unavoidable. However, this adult is put in the position of demanding the respect and deference that are due authority figures without having made a commitment to the child. It is unfair to the child to attempt to parent him if one is unwilling to make a commitment to that child or to the child's parent.

For the child whose parents have divorced, the unspeakable has already happened: the integrity of the home and of the parent–child relationship has been destroyed in a way that is not supposed to happen. This loss of integrity is significant for the child no matter what age. The child will be growing up in a home in which he cannot count on both parents being there for him and for each other. To ask a child to trust and obey another adult who has not been able to make a commitment to him is to set oneself up for very difficult authority struggles.

How is the child to regard this live-in partner? He or she is not a parent or stepparent. Is he or she a roommate? This places the adult at a level equal to that of the child. In fact, the child can see himself as being in a superior position to the adult, since he has both a biological and a legal tie to his parent, which the live-in partner does not. The adult with no commitment to the child becomes the child's competitor for the parent's affection and time, with no legitimate claim to be in that position.

This is the ambiguous position parents put their children in when they choose to live in this way. It becomes particularly problematic with the challenges to authority that children with ADHD often pose. When parents in this situation come to me with these dilemmas about authority, I believe it is my responsibility to be honest with them about the ambiguity that their choices set up for them and the child. I try to take an educative approach, not condemning the parent, but simply doing my job to make him or her aware of the problems inherent in the situation that cannot simply be fixed with behavior management techniques.

CUSTODIAL ARRANGEMENTS

Courts consider a wide range of custodial arrangements. They are concerned about being fair and equitable to both parents. In the interest of giving equal consideration to the child's relationship to both parents, the courts often agree to arrangements that tax the organizational skills of the parents and the child. In considering the best arrangement for the child with ADHD, his ability to organize both time and his physical belongings needs to be taken into account.

One popular arrangement is shared physical custody, with the child alternating between each parent's home on a nightly basis. Many parents prefer this because it gives them an equal amount of time with the child both during the week and over the weekend, and allows each parent to participate equally in the day-to-day life of the child.

Parents considering such an arrangement for their ADHD child are cautioned to consider the organizational demands that this makes on their child. The child will have to continually ask himself: "Which bus do I take home from school today?" The child will be in constant peril of leaving important schoolbooks, sports equipment, or clothing at the wrong parent's house on the wrong day. This increases not only the child's confusion but also the possibility of conflict between the parents.

I have often heard parents complaining that one parent did not send the child back to them with the same clothes in which he arrived, or with the appropriate books or equipment. The children, often without the materials they need to do their homework, find themselves with more incomplete work than previously, or staying up later to do their homework because one parent has to retrieve the assignment or book from the other's house.

Sadly for parents, the best custodial arrangement for the child with ADHD is often one that leaves one parent with more time to spend with the child than the other. Regularity and consistency are so important to the child with ADHD that it is helpful to have a home base or a primary residence. This is comforting to the child and helps him feel and be organized. Some parents arrange to switch off every week, which provides the child with more consistency than switching off every day.

Parents often need help in putting their own needs aside and seeing objectively what is best for their child. Problem solving with a chart can make things more concrete for them. Each parent can list the different custodial arrangements, the advantages and disadvantages to them, and the advantages and disadvantages to the child. They then will have the big picture and more information on which to base their decision:

Custodial arrangement	Advantages to me	Disadvantages to me	Advantages to child	Disadvantages to child

❖ CHAPTER 10 ❖

To Medicate or Not to Medicate

ATTITUDES TOWARD MEDICATION

Many parents begin their assessment with me by saying emphatically, "I am not going to put my child on *drugs*!" The last word is emphasized and pronounced as if it were an obscenity. I hear this statement often before I have even begun the assessment process, before I have any idea what the child's condition is and what possible treatments might be appropriate.

Many parents have a negative reaction to the idea of medication for ADHD that they do not have to medication for other medical conditions. I sometimes ask the parent, if their child had diabetes and needed insulin, would they deprive him of that medication? I explain to them that, to the best of our knowledge, ADHD is a condition that involves the inefficient regulation of certain chemicals in the body, which, in that way, makes it similar to diabetes. I explain to them that I can understand their hesitation to have their child take medication, and I explain to them what I know of the research and what I have seen in my clinical experience. It is my job to give them information so that they can make the best informed decision possible for their child. I try to explore where their negative impression of medication has come from.

I further tell the parents that I am not a medical doctor and I have no interest in selling them on medication. Furthermore, if the question of medication seems to be relevant after the evaluation has been completed, they should have a conversation with their child's doctor, who is the professional who would be most knowledgeable about medication, and the only one who is qualified to fully explain the potential benefits and risks.

The parents should have the following information:

- Stimulants have been used in the treatment of children with ADHD for more than twenty-five years, and no significant long-term side effects have been discovered.
- Stimulant medication helps between 70 and 90 percent of children with ADHD (Barkley 1995).
- The stimulants are short-acting. That is, they may be effective for three to six hours, and are out of the body within twenty-four hours (Barkley 1995). If parents do not like what they do, they can be discontinued and the effect will stop.
- We know fairly quickly if the stimulants are helping significantly. They do not take days or weeks to build up in the body, but rather are effective in less than an hour of taking them.
- We might have to try different doses of a medication to see if it is effective or if the child is getting the maximum help from that medication.
- If the stimulants do not help, there are other medications that are being used to treat ADHD. These medications might not have as good a track record as the stimulants do, and might have other side effects or medical risks that should be considered. However, many can be very effective with minimal risk.
- Currently, the most preferred treatment for ADHD involves a combination of medication and behavior management.

SORTING OUT ONE'S BELIEFS

It would be wise to help parents sort out their biases about medication from what they know to be true. They might want to make a list of their beliefs and questions and check them out with their child's doctor. It is best if both parents attend the meeting with the doctor, so they both have the opportunity to ask questions and express doubts. There is no substitute for being there. It is much better than relying on one's spouse or ex-spouse to explain what the doctor said, and then putting the spouse or ex-spouse in the untenable position of having to deal with one's doubts about a subject on which he or she is not an expert.

My questions for the doctor	The doctor's responses

After the meeting with the doctor, the parents should sit down with each other, discuss their thoughts and feelings, and try to separate their biases from the facts. They might want to list the potential benefits and risks in order to weigh them better.

Benefits	**Risks**

COMPLICATED CASES

The question of medication can be complicated. There are many children diagnosed with ADHD who have characteristics that have long been seen as common in ADHD children but are not part of the diagnostic criteria, such as having extreme difficulty regulating their emotions and their internal state. Many of these children are depressed, and many are unusually and persistently irritable. Their parents report that, not matter how firm and consistent they are in responding to their children's behavior, their children overreact emotionally, and have tantrums for unusual periods of time. Some of these children spend most of the day being negative, angry, or irritable. Others seem to be emotionally shut down. They don't interact much with others and they make many self-deprecating comments. These are children who, although they meet the diagnostic criteria for ADHD, might have affective disorders in addition to ADHD, which might actually be causing some of the problems associated with ADHD. It is also possible that some of these children have been misdiagnosed, and their symptoms are due to an affective disorder rather than to ADHD. However, many of them are likely to have dual diagnoses. In addition to ADHD, these children might be depressed, or have a childhood form of bipolar disorder, in which the prominent symptom is irritability rather than the mania that is commonly seen in adults with this disorder.

There are other children who are predominantly anxious rather than depressed. These children might have some form of social phobia, agoraphobia, or separation anxiety. Some seem to have a free-floating anxiety that hits them whenever they are in a new or unfamiliar situation, or with a lot of people, or away from home. I have seen adolescents who will not attend school for days at a time. They say they don't feel well, or dissolve in tears when their parents try to get them out of the house, or drive them to school and try to get them out of the car. The parents will work out special arrangements with the school guidance counselor. If the child gets into the school building, he might spend a lot of the time in the counselor's office or the nurse's office.

Because of the parents' experience over time with the child's ADHD symptoms, many of them respond as they would to any oppositional and defiant behavior. They try to enforce limits and, often, the child becomes more upset and anxious. In these situations, the parents should be alert to the possibility that their child could have an anxiety disorder along with or instead of ADHD. These anxiety disorders have a biological component that results in dysregulation of the child's emotional state. The child might very well be and feel anxious and be unable to control the anxiety.

Complicating the picture is the issue of secondary gain. The power the child gains from having these symptoms—power over his parents, over the demands made on him, over going to school, over being indulged and attended to—can have a reinforcing effect on his behavior, exacerbating his anxiety-related symptoms. The parents then can find it very confusing to sort out what is biologically based anxiety and what is learned or manipulative. In these cases, I recommend that the parents pursue a medication evaluation, but that they also give the child the consistent message that they expect him to go to school and cope with his anxiety in school. They should work out a plan with the guidance counselor, the principal, and perhaps the truancy officer to get the child into the school building.

These children need a good medication evaluation by someone who is familiar with ADHD, childhood affective disorders, and their overlap. I encourage parents to discuss medication with their child's pediatrician, and to get a referral to a child psychiatrist if the pediatrician is not experienced in prescribing in these types of cases.

❖ CHAPTER 11 ❖

Is My Child Getting the Help He or She Needs?

Now that parents have made decisions regarding the management of their child's behavior, their relationship with their child, their child's school program, and medication, how do they know if any of this is benefiting their child?

It is a good idea for parents to keep track of how their child is doing on a regular basis in a way that allows them to compare his behavior at different points in time. To track the child's behavior, it would be helpful to make use of rating scales that measure it in different settings. At home, there are several situations in which ADHD children commonly have trouble attending. *The Home Situations Questionnaire–Revised (HSQ-R)*, which was developed by G. J. DuPaul (1990), is a tool that is often used by professionals to get a reading of which situations create the most difficulty for these children. It gives a baseline reading of the child's difficulties before treatment begins, and then can be used weekly or monthly to see if there is improvement.

If there is no improvement in important areas over time, it probably is time to reevaluate what the parents and clinician are doing and see if a change of treatment is called for. If there is improvement in some areas but not in others, this questionnaire can pinpoint the areas that need more work.

Home Situations Questionnaire–Revised

Name of Child ______________________ Date __________

Name of Person Completing This Form ______________________

Does this child have problems paying attention or concentrating in any of these situations? If so, indicate how severe these attentional difficulties are.

Situations	*Yes/No* (Circle one)		*If yes, how severe?* (Circle one) Mild								Severe
While playing alone	Yes	No	1	2	3	4	5	6	7	8	9
While playing with other children	Yes	No	1	2	3	4	5	6	7	8	9
Mealtimes	Yes	No	1	2	3	4	5	6	7	8	9
Getting dressed	Yes	No	1	2	3	4	5	6	7	8	9
While watching TV	Yes	No	1	2	3	4	5	6	7	8	9
When visitors are in your home	Yes	No	1	2	3	4	5	6	7	8	9
When you are visiting someone else	Yes	No	1	2	3	4	5	6	7	8	9
At church or Sunday school	Yes	No	1	2	3	4	5	6	7	8	9
In supermarkets, stores, restaurants, or other public areas	Yes	No	1	2	3	4	5	6	7	8	9
When asked to do chores at home	Yes	No	1	2	3	4	5	6	7	8	9
During conversations with others	Yes	No	1	2	3	4	5	6	7	8	9
While in the car	Yes	No	1	2	3	4	5	6	7	8	9
When father is home	Yes	No	1	2	3	4	5	6	7	8	9
When asked to do school homework	Yes	No	1	2	3	4	5	6	7	8	9

(Reprinted with permission from *The Home and School Situations Questionnaires–Revised: Normative Data, Reliability, and Validity*, 1990 by George J. DuPaul, Ph.D.)

A simpler monitoring system can look like this:

Attention problems at home			
Week of:			
Morning routine	mild	moderate	severe
Doing homework	mild	moderate	severe
At the dinner table	mild	moderate	severe
Complying with requests	mild	moderate	severe
Bedtime routine	mild	moderate	severe
Playing with friends	mild	moderate	severe
In public places	mild	moderate	severe

If the parents prefer to use a numerical scale instead of the designations *mild*, *moderate*, and *severe*, they can create this chart with a 1–5 or 1–10 scale. Comparing the ratings on a weekly basis will give the clinician or parents some sense of whether the child is improving.

It also makes sense to set up a similar monitoring system at school and use a form that is quick and easy for the teacher to fill out. *The School Situations Questionnaire–Revised (SSQ-R)*, also developed by DuPaul (1990) is similar to the *HSQ-R* in that it identifies common school situations and quantifies the teacher's impression of the amount of difficulty the student has paying attention. The teacher can complete this form at the end of every week or two weeks:

School Situations Questionnaire–Revised

Name of Child ____

Name of Person Completing This Form ______________________________

Does this child have problems paying attention or concentrating in any of these situations? If so, indicate how severe these attentional difficulties are.

Situations	*Yes/No* (Circle one)		*If yes, how severe?* Mild			(Circle one)					Severe
During individual deskwork	Yes	No	1	2	3	4	5	6	7	8	9
During small-group activities	Yes	No	1	2	3	4	5	6	7	8	9
During free-play time in class	Yes	No	1	2	3	4	5	6	7	8	9
During lectures to the class	Yes	No	1	2	3	4	5	6	7	8	9
On field trips	Yes	No	1	2	3	4	5	6	7	8	9
During special assemblies	Yes	No	1	2	3	4	5	6	7	8	9
During movies, filmstrips	Yes	No	1	2	3	4	5	6	7	8	9
During class discussions	Yes	No	1	2	3	4	5	6	7	8	9

(Reprinted with permission from *The Home and School Situations Questionnaires–Revised: Normative Data, Reliability, and Validity*, 1990 by George J. DuPaul, Ph.D.)

In this case, too, the parents can develop their own scale if that is more convenient. The advantage of this is that it can be tailored to the needs and the behaviors of each particular child. A sample one might look like this:

Attention and behavior problems at school			
Week of:			
Working at his desk	mild	moderate	severe
Listening to teacher	mild	moderate	severe
During transitions	mild	moderate	severe
At recess	mild	moderate	severe
At lunch	mild	moderate	severe
During tests	mild	moderate	severe
During physical education	mild	moderate	severe
Entering school in the morning	mild	moderate	severe
Leaving school	mild	moderate	severe

Again, this can be adapted to a 5- or 10-point scale.

The parents might also want to develop a scale to monitor the symptoms of ADHD in order to track their course over time or to monitor the effects of medication on specific symptoms or behaviors. Since each child is different, the parents can design one with their child in mind, to be used by them and/or by the child's teacher or teachers. The parents can select from the *DSM-IV* list of symptoms (see Chapter 2) those that pertain to their child or paraphrase them for the purpose of simplicity, and monitor their frequency at home or at school.

Symptom	**Never**	**Sometimes**	**Often**
Makes careless mistakes			
Does not seem to listen			
Does not finish work or chores			
Has difficulty with organization			
Easily distracted			
Often fidgets or squirms			
Has difficulty waiting his turn			

❖ CHAPTER 12 ❖

Parents Ask: Can I Be a Better Parent?

After the parents go through this guidebook and complete some of these exercises, which can increase their understanding of their child and give them some insight into themselves as parents, they can then assess where they can improve themselves. They must be honest about facing their shortcomings. They can solicit input from someone who is familiar with their parenting skills, such as friend or relative. They should ask for honesty, not compliments, and accept what they are told graciously. The parents can then list their strengths and weaknesses, and decide which weaknesses they want to change.

Strengths	Weaknesses

Each parent can choose one weakness to work on improving, one that can be improved in the short term. This might not be the most important one to start with, but the parents should give themselves an experience of success in order to motivate themselves to continue to make changes.

They can assess the seriousness of their weaknesses by considering how much each interferes with their parenting and their relationship with their child and spouse. This is similar to rating the seriousness of their child's behavior problems. They probably considered how much disruption each of their child's problems caused. They can rate the weaknesses on a scale of 1 to 3, with 1 being "mild," 2 being "moderate," and 3 being "severe." They can write this rating on the right hand side in the form above. For example, if one of the weaknesses is "impatience," and the parent finds he has little tolerance for any childlike behavior in the evening, to the point where he quickly escalates to yelling and screaming almost every night, the parent might want to rate this weakness a 3. If the parent gives his child a time-out almost every time the child speaks to him disrespectfully, but every five times or so the parent ends up yelling at the child or failing to follow through with the time-out, he might rate this weakness, "inconsistency with time-out," with a 1.

For the first attempt at improvement, the parent should choose a weakness that he rated 1 or 2, something that occurs fairly frequently so that he can monitor it on a daily or almost daily basis. For example, if the parent loses patience with the children in the car, but he only drives them places once every two weeks, this would probably not be a good problem to start with.

Once a weakness is chosen, the parent should establish his goal in a positive way, being as specific as possible. For example, if the problem is "impatience," identifying the goal as "don't lose my cool" puts the desired behavior in negative terms; it tells the parent what he shouldn't do. Using the phrase "be more patient" puts it in positive terms, but is not very specific. A positive, more specific goal would be "keep calm during the bedtime routine and speak in a firm but controlled voice."

The parent can then write down his goal and monitor either the number of times his behavior succeeded in reaching his goal or the amount of time in which his behavior conformed to his goal. Some behaviors and situations lend themselves more to the first way of monitoring, and some are easier to keep track of the second way. With this particular goal, it probably makes sense to monitor the amount of time that the parent remained calm and kept his voice under control. A related goal for this parent could be "walk out of the room when getting too angry." This would have him remove himself from the situation whenever he was on the verge of losing control, returning when he collected himself. This behavior could be monitored by the frequency of its occurrence and by the number of times the parent did not succeed and allowed himself to lose control with the children.

A daily self-monitoring chart for these behaviors could look like this:

Goal: Keep calm during the bedtime routine and speak in a firm but controlled voice.

Date	1–10 mins.	11–20 mins.	21–30 mins.	31–40 mins.	41–50 mins.	51–60 mins.

Goal: Walk out of the room when too angry.

Date	# of times too angry	# of times left room

For every ten-minute period that the first goal is met, the parent can simply place a check in the appropriate box. For every time the parent becomes too angry, and for each of those times that he leaves the room, he can check the appropriate boxes. The parent can now monitor his progress on a daily basis.

THE PARENTS' ANGER

No matter how rational parents try to be, emotions get in their way. But emotions are good things. They warn us of danger and they give us important information about what is going on inside of us. Emotions get parents into trouble when they are out of balance with reason and logic. Men often complain that women are "too emotional." What they seem to mean by this is that they believe women often allow their emotional reactions to influence their behavior at the expense of logical long-term goals. Men often pride themselves on being able to put their emotions on the back burner and carry out a plan without getting sidetracked or manipulated. However, there is one emotion with which men are often quite irrational without realizing it. That emotion is anger. Of course, both men and women feel anger and are capable of becoming irrational when in its grip. It is very important, therefore, for parents to take control of their anger and not have it rule them. If it does rule them, they will be locked into control struggles with their children with no way out. There are three forms of anger that parents need to be aware of: anger toward their children, anger toward their spouses, and anger toward other things that get displaced onto their children or their spouses. Let's take the last one first.

Misplaced Anger

Parents can imagine this scenario:

> Think about times that you come home from work upset or frustrated about something that happened there. You feel depleted of energy, and the kids, on the other hand, are abundantly energetic and demanding. In this state, the children are not very good at listening and you know that you will have to repeat yourself several times. The scene that greets you at home is not unusual except that you are angry and feel a need to control things and to lash out at anyone or anything that makes your life difficult.
>
> In this mood, you can become a monster to your children, who might be puzzled and cowed by your anger, but will not be able to understand it. You might regret your actions and words the next day when you are calmer, and regret the damage that you might have done to your relationship with your children, but at the moment, you cannot seem to prevent yourself from lashing out at them.

There are four things for parents to think about (1) situations in which they most often take out on the children the anger felt toward other things, (2) how parents can signal to themselves that they are in one of those situations where they are vulnerable to being irrationally angry, (3) what they can do to handle the situation differently, and (4) what signal one parent can give to the other that he is heading down the wrong track. Examples of problem situations are coming home from work after a hard day; being moody after getting off the phone with a relative who has insulted, criticized, not listened to, or manipulated him; having an angry interchange with his spouse; or having financial worries. The parent needs to be aware that this is a problem situation and tell himself, "I am probably upset and I don't want to take it out on my kids," or "I know I am short tempered, so I will try to take it easy on my kids tonight," or "I need a moment to calm down before I go into the house because I don't want to blow up at the kids." The parent can consider doing things differently by (1) walking out of the room, (2) allowing his spouse to take over some responsibility, (3) taking a moment to do some deep breathing or splashing cold water on her face, or (4) making a game out of the interaction. Signals that a spouse can give should be prearranged during a calm moment so there is no misunderstanding as to what the spouse means or the other spouse's intent to help him. They can include a hand signal that only the two or them know, a comment, such as "Take five, dear," or an affectionate hug.

The parent might want to write these things down in the form of a chart that he can keep handy:

Anger-causing situations	Signals to myself	What I can do differently	Signals from my spouse

There is another type of misplaced anger that is much harder to recognize or to change: anger that comes from years back, left over from childhood, and involving ways in which the parent was wronged, neglected, or mistreated that he or she might not even be aware of. Harboring anger or resentment from the past is a difficult thing to get a handle on. Signs that this might be the case are usually noticed by other people more easily than by the individual. Some questions that the parent might ask himself are:

Do I find myself getting angry a lot, more than most people? (Y/N)

Do little things often get me angry? (Y/N)

Do I often feel bad about how angry I was, after the fact? (Y/N)

Does my spouse feel that my anger is out of proportion to the situations that get me angry? (Y/N)

Does my spouse or my best friend think that I have an anger problem? (Y/N)

Do my spouse, my children, or other people feel that they have to "walk on eggshells" when they are around me, to prevent me from getting angry? (Y/N)

If parents answered "Yes" to any of these questions, they might have an anger problem that is a holdover from the past. The anger might be out of proportion to present reality, and therefore might be fueled by past hurts. If they have difficulty figuring out the causes of their irrational anger, or controlling it, counseling might help.

Anger toward One's Children

Thinking through a typical day or week, a parent might recognize a pattern in which she repeatedly gets angry at her children during certain times or in certain situations. Some situations might simply just "push her buttons," and some recognition and planning might help her to control it without the need for psychotherapy. A parent might, for example, become especially outraged when the kids are acting up in the car and she is trying to drive, or when they dawdle during their morning or bedtime routines, or when they eat with their hands at dinner. After identifying these problem areas, the parent can try to turn these situations into productive interactions. For example, if she ends up yelling and screaming in the car a lot, she might use a think ahead/think aloud strategy the next time that she is about to get into the car with the children. She might say, "You know that I often get mad at you for your behavior when I'm driving. I want you to be able to follow a couple of rules in the car: no shouting, because that can scare me and cause an accident, and no fighting, because that can distract me and cause an accident. Now repeat to me what the rules are . . . Good! Now if I feel that your behavior is getting out of control, I will give you one warning and I expect you to listen. What will I do when your behavior is getting bad? . . . Good! Then what will you do? . . . Good. If you listen to me and your behavior is good, you will be able to (watch your tape, play with your game, have your friend over, etc.) when we get home. If you do not listen, you will have a time-out as soon as we get to where we're going, and you will lose your privileges for the rest of the afternoon."

The parent can identify the situations in which she typically gets angry at her children. Then she can start with one situation that both occurs frequently (such as on a daily basis or several times a week) and which she has a reasonably good chance of handling successfully. Then she can write down what she wants to do to change it. She can work at the problem for a week and record the number of times that the situation turned out better than it had in the past. If there are more times in which the parent is more satisfied than in the past, then she is successfully changing the situation and should congratulate herself.

Situations that get me angry with the children

The situation that I want to change first is: ___________________________

What I will do to change it is:

Week of	Number of times situation occurred	Number of times it turned out better	Number of times it turned out the same

Anger toward One's Spouse

Parents might get into repeated conflicts with each other that make it hard for them to parent together; thus, by default, they give their children control of the household. Many couples get into repetitive, petty arguments that appear silly when they are looked at later on. There are situations in which one's feelings are easily hurt and a person is therefore unable to see beyond his hurt and deal with a situation effectively. In these situations, couples often fight about who is right or who is wrong rather than about what is best to do to resolve it.

There might be times and situations that involve parenting in which one's anger repeatedly comes up. If the anger gets in the way of managing the children's behavior effectively, it is important for the two parents to find some way to resolve this problem. The parents might decide to switch off whose method to use, or they might decide to go with the way one of them wants to do things for a specified period of time, such as a week, and see how it turns out. They might both be able to compromise and find a method that is not perfect, but that they both can live with.

The parents can start with lists of those situations in which they repeatedly get angry at each other for child-related issues. The situations that elicit this anger might be the same for both parents or there might be some differences. Then the parents should agree on one situation to start with that they want to do differently. They should not choose the situation that will be the most difficult to change. They should choose one that they have a reasonably good chance of changing. Once they have experienced success with a more manageable problem, then it makes sense to tackle a more difficult one.

Once they have selected the problem to start with, they can decide what they will change to make the situation better. They should agree on a time frame and a way that they will know whether it is working. Afterward, they can assess whether the situation is better or not.

Situations that get me mad at my spouse

Situations that get my spouse mad at me

The situation we will work at changing first is: ______________________

What we will do differently is:

Week of	Number of times situation occurred	Number of times it turned out better	Number of times it turned out the same

After the agreed-upon period of time for review, if the situation did not improve, the parents can think of what the two of them have to do differently to fine tune their approach. Then they can try it for another week or month and review it again. Once they have changed the situation to their mutual satisfaction, they can choose a second problem to work on in a similar way.

WHAT PARENTS CAN LEARN FROM AND TEACH EACH OTHER

Fathers are often good at disciplining without getting sidetracked or manipulated by their child's emotional displays. They are often skilled at putting their emotions on the back burner. However, this ability often leads them to neglect their child's emotional state and emotional needs to the point where it makes them less effective, for example, knowing where the line is that separates punishment from ridicule, or assuming that all crying is manipulation and failing to respond to the child's genuine distress.

Mothers are often more emotionally in tune with their children, and understand the types of consequences, both positive and negative, that are most likely to be effective with them. They are often better at balancing criticism with praise, and they can be better at punishing their children without ridiculing them. However, the flip side of this strength is that increased emotional understanding makes one vulnerable to negotiating too much with the child, or to softening the punishment at the first sign of the child's unhappiness.

Earlier in this book, parents assessed their strengths and weaknesses. One parent's strengths might be characteristics that the spouse can learn from to become a better parent. On the other hand, one's weaknesses might be traits that one's spouse is especially strong in. Parents can compare their lists of strengths and weaknesses. They can choose items in which one of them is strong and the other is relatively weak. They might decide to teach each other, and learn from each other, how to be stronger in the areas in which one of them is weak and the other is strong. They can decide how they will learn from and teach each other, through observation, constructive feedback, or the practice of certain behaviors with the other person's supervision.

My strengths	My weaknesses

My spouse's strengths	My spouse's weaknesses

What I will teach my spouse	Methods we will use	Number of times my spouse showed improved skills	Number of times my spouse handled things the old way

What my spouse will teach me	Methods we will use	Number of times I showed improved skills	Number of times I handled things the old way

The parents can set up a schedule of times they will meet to review their progress and fine tune their teaching methods.

Renee was the parent who usually helped her daughter Sonia with homework every night. Sonia was an unusually headstrong girl who had ADHD. She liked to do things on her own, even when she was frustrated with her efforts. In fact, the more frustrated she became, the more adamantly she resisted any help from her mother. Her attempts to do her homework were punctuated with frequent groans and pounding on the table. Renee would often come in and inquire about what was the matter. Although Renee had become better at entering the room slowly and gently, instead of rushing in as she formerly did, Sonia still reacted forcefully.

Sonia's reactions were confusing for Renee because they seemed to communicate both a desperate cry for help and a rejection of it at the same time. Renee tried to sympathize with Sonia's frustration, but Sonia only responded that her mother did not understand and could not help her. Desperate to help, Renee tried to go over the homework with Sonia, but Sonia had already shut down and could not listen.

If Renee ended up trying to force Sonia to get back to business, it usually led to an escalation of the conflict, with mother yelling at daughter and daughter crying.

In reviewing Renee's strengths and weaknesses with her husband, Ted, they agreed that she had a very good understanding of Sonia's emotional needs, her poor self-esteem, and her tendency to become easily overwhelmed. At times, she was effective at helping Sonia soothe herself and calm down. She was also very patient with Sonia and did not prematurely try to force her to do something she was not ready to do. They also agreed that Renee had difficulty judging when to end the interaction with Sonia and walk away or set a limit.

Ted, on the other hand, had little patience for Sonia's "histrionics," which often exacerbated them rather than facilitating Sonia's soothing. He was effective, however, in setting limits when he decided that it was time to do so. He could do this calmly and firmly, and follow through without backing down or second thoughts.

Assessing their strengths and weaknesses led Renee to develop the following chart:

My strengths	**My weaknesses**
Good teacher	Yell and scream when out of ideas
Patient	Too patient—delay putting my foot down and setting limits
Understand Sonia's emotional needs	Not effective at ending control struggles once they start
Can approach Sonia gently	
Can help Sonia calm down	

My spouse's strengths	**My spouse's weaknesses**
Firm and consistent with limits	Impatient with emotional displays
Follows through with limits once they are set	Can set limits too soon and too harshly to be effective
Remains calm when limits are challenged	Not available consistently to work on homework
Does not doubt or question himself	

After reviewing these charts, Ted and Renee decided that Ted would make it his goal to be there for homework help 75 percent of the time, that they would alternate evenings in which each of them began to work with Sonia, that they would first try to calm and soothe her at her first signs of distress, and that if the initial attempt at limit setting failed, Ted would enforce the limit if he was home. If Ted was not home, Renee would enforce the limit and would get coaching from Ted as to how to do it unemotionally. Ted, on the other hand, would receive coaching from Renee as to how to avoid control struggles when he is trying to soothe Sonia and get her back on task.

QUANTITY TIME

Overstressed and overworked parents talk about the virtues of quality time. Since parents don't have much time to spend with their children, they try to justify the little time they do have by labeling it "quality time." By this they mean that when they are with the children, they plan interesting or exciting things to do. By saying this, they imply that simply hanging out with their children, spending time together just for the sake of spending time together, and doing mundane activities like grocery shopping or eating are wastes of time. But "quantity time" might be even more important than "quality time." If parents are not spending time with their child, they are giving him or her the message that the child is not as important as other things that they value.

Furthermore, young children relate to the world largely through how their daily physical needs—food, clothing, shelter, health, and cleanliness—are met. Parents meet these needs by changing diapers, rocking the child to sleep, feeding the child, and guiding and helping the child through the morning and evening routines, which are not just trivial tasks to be done by hired caregivers. Rather, they allow the child to experience basic trust in the world, and experience how the world will meet their needs or frustrate them. Children learn that they can count on the world and count on their own bodies to serve them well. By having their daily physical needs met reliably, children also experience the predictability and reliability of their actions and of the responses from the environment ("If I take this much time getting dressed, I'll have less time to eat." "If I wear this, I'll freeze." "If I do these things in order, I'll get them done more quickly."). Also important in this process is experiencing the ability to interact with authority to get their needs met, and the attainment of mastery over self-care.

Parents can think of the value of arranging their work schedules to have dinner with their children on a regular basis, to participate in putting their children to bed, and to be home with their children just for the sake of being with them. Parents should consider how much time they spend with the child. What are the opportunities they take advantage of or miss? It might help to keep track of the time they spend with their child and set goals for increasing it.

Time of day	Spent with child
Morning routine	
Coming home from school	
Dinner	
Homework	
After dinner	
Bedtime routine	
Weekend errands	
Sports practices and games	
After-school activities and events	
Weekend recreational activities	

Parents can select a time or times that they can arrange their schedules to spend more time with their child. They can set a goal as to how many more time periods they will spend with their child in the following week.

SUPPORT FOR PARENTS

Out of shame or a need to protect their privacy, many parents choose to go it alone rather than seek out support and help from others. They don't want others to know their business, especially their failures, and they don't believe others can help them. Unfortunately, these feelings often result in parents not getting support that might be helpful to them.

In addition to the support they get from clinicians, parents need support in the community. It is important to assess if parents are getting that support. Are their friends and families supportive of their efforts to discipline their children? Do the grandparents and other family members back them up or undermine their efforts? Are uncooperative family members educable? Can they be brought on board as part of the team? Do the parents know any other parents who have similar struggles with their own children? Do the parents know about and take advantage of support groups and organizations such as Ch.A.D.D. (Children and Adults with Attention Deficit Disorder)? Do the parents know about resources offered by organizations such as Ch.A.D.D., the ADDA (Attention Deficit Disorders Association), or the LDA (Learning Disabilities Association)? Do the parents have access to on-line chat groups and bulletin boards?

Parents who believe they are doing okay might, after looking at their support or nonsupport systems, realize that they would benefit from more support and more helpful input. After looking at all the negative influences they have to cope with, they might decide to become more assertive in dealing with their extended families or to spend less time with people who undermine their efforts.

❖ CHAPTER 13 ❖

Parents Ask: Could I Have ADHD?

Often, in my first interview with parents whose child I am assessing for ADHD, the mother will recount in great detail all of the difficulties and misdeeds of her child over the years. If the father has sat there quietly until the mother has finished, I will turn to him and ask: "Do you see things the same way or differently?" He is likely to say, "I think he's perfectly normal. He's just like I was when I was a boy!" If I encourage him to continue, I will often get stories of hair-raising adventures as a youth, acting up in school, and failure to finish school or achieve up to his potential. Shortly after that, the mother will often request that her husband be evaluated when I am finished evaluating their child.

Mothers sometimes embarrassed tell me that they were singled out for socializing too much in class, or were bored or uninterested in school. They often failed to earn good grades in school until high school or college. It has been estimated that, if a child has ADHD, there is about a 25 percent chance that at least one of his parents has ADHD. Parents seem to know when their ADHD child is like one of them, although it is often hard for them to ask for help and acknowledge how ADHD is still impacting on their lives. The symptoms that are listed in the diagnostic manual were mostly written with children in mind, but they can be applied to adults. The clinician can present the list of symptoms to the parents verbally or in writing, and ask them to indicate whether these characteristics occur often in their adult life. A person who knows them well can provide his observations about the frequency of these behaviors at present. Then a person who knew the parent well as a child, such as a parent, a sibling, or a close relative, can respond to the symptoms according to what the parent was like as a child.

Attention Deficit Hyperactivity Disorder Symptoms

	Yes	No
Inattention		
often fails to give close attention to details or makes careless mistakes in schoolwork, work, or other activities		
often has difficulty sustaining attention in tasks		
often does not seem to listen when spoken to directly		
often does not follow through on instructions and fails to finish schoolwork, chores, or duties in the workplace (not due to oppositional behavior or failure to understand instructions)		
often has difficulty organizing tasks and activities		
often avoids, dislikes, or is reluctant to engage in tasks that require sustained mental effort (such as schoolwork or homework)		
often loses things necessary for tasks or activities		
is often distracted by extraneous stimuli		
is often forgetful in daily activities		

Hyperactivity-Impulsivity

often fidgets with hands or feet or squirms in seat

often leaves seat in classroom or in other situations in which remaining seated is expected

subjective feelings of restlessness

often has difficulty engaging in leisure activities quietly

is often "on the go" or often acts as if "driven by a motor"

often talks excessively

often blurts out answers before questions have been completed

often has difficulty awaiting turn

often interrupts or intrudes on others (e.g., butts into conversations)

The first nine items are symptoms of inattention, and the second nine items are symptoms of hyperactivity-impulsivity. A diagnosis requires six symptoms in either category occurring more frequently than in others of the same age. These criteria were formulated with children in mind. Since the symptoms often decrease in severity and number over time, ADHD adults might have fewer symptoms than do ADHD children. It is also important to note that, for ADHD to be diagnosed, it must have existed in childhood, being evident before the age of 7, with symptoms such as inattention, impulsivity, and hyperactivity, at levels greater than would be normal for this age group; there also had to be the required number of symptoms occurring frequently to have made a diagnosis, and the symptoms had to interfere with important areas of functioning in the child's life.

Once the existence of the syndrome in childhood is reasonably established (and this can be difficult to know for sure, as people's memories fade, and people were not as aware of the syndrome years ago as they are now), to make the diagnosis there has to be a determination that the symptoms persist into adulthood. There is no commonly agreed-upon required number of symptoms.

If the parent looks at his adulthood ratings and sees a total of four or more symptoms in either group (inattention or hyperactivity-impulsivity), the parent has cause for concern about ADHD. But it is important that the parent not diagnose himself. This exercise is only intended to increase the parent's awareness of possible symptoms. The parent should consult with a qualified professional if he suspects that he might have ADHD. There are several conditions that look like ADHD, so even if the parent has a high number of symptoms, he should not automatically assume that they are caused by ADHD.

It is also important for a parent to consider whether he could have ADHD, because an ADHD parent raising an ADHD child presents a more difficult situation. It is like standing in a hall of mirrors, looking at one's reflection endlessly bouncing back at oneself. To cope with the child's impulsivity, the parent must deal with his own. The same goes for anger problems, distractibility, and restlessness.

If a parent believes that he might have ADHD, he should be evaluated, but he will probably either be resistant to the idea or procrastinate. The parent should set a goal by when he will (1) get a referral to a psychologist or a physician, and (2) make an appointment. In preparation for the appointment, he should list the problems he has and how long they have lasted. A spouse or friend can provide input on this.

Signs and symptoms	Occurred in childhood or adulthood?	How long did it last?

By getting the help that he needs, the parent will help his child get the parenting the child needs.

❖ CHAPTER 14 ❖

The Parenting Scorecard

This is an opportunity for parents to review the goals they have set, the progress they have made, and the work they have left to do. It is also a good time for them to take stock of what they have learned about themselves, what they have learned about their spouses, and what they have learned about their children.

The parents and their therapist can look back over the work they have done in this book. What goals have they set? What progress have they made toward those goals?

Goals we have set	Progress we have made

What I have learned about myself

What I have learned about my child

What I have learned about my spouse	What my spouse has learned about me

Is life better for these parents than it was before they began this guidebook? If their answer is yes, then this has been a worthwhile journey and the parents should be congratulated for taking it. They must remember that parenting the child with ADHD requires constant effort, learning, and improvement. They must keep up the work they are doing.

Parents will probably find that several strategies work for a while and then stop working well. The temptation will be to give up and abandon their efforts. Parents must keep in mind that with the ADHD child, things can get old pretty fast and might need to be changed fairly often. The ADHD child has a strong need for novelty. If something stops working, it means that it's time to fine tune it or to try something new. If something was working for a while, it proves that the parents were doing something effective and that their methods are sound. The fact that something that previously worked is no longer effective does not mean that the parents are ineffective. Just the opposite. Parents need help in seeing that what they perceive as failures might actually have been short-term successes.

Effective parents know that things change and they have to change with them. For example, two parents told me that they put their child's morning routine on a chart, so instead of having to remind the child numerous times to complete each task of his morning routine every morning, they referred him to his chart and rewarded him for completing his routine without undue delay. The problem was that this chart held the child's interest or attention only for one week. I suggested that the parents keep the chart method, but that they build in novelty in two ways: (1) they change the color of the chart each week by using different colors of bright, fluorescent poster board, and (2) they mix up the sequence of behaviors in the routine each week.

This guidebook can be referred to as one's situation changes over time. Parents and therapists can use these exercises to help parents rework their solutions and to rethink their understanding of their child, themselves, and their spouse.

❖ CHAPTER 15 ❖

Coming to Terms with the Parents' Own Parents

INFLUENCES FROM THE PAST

Some parents practice and practice new methods and techniques, and try new ways of understanding how they are parenting their children, and they still find themselves stuck in old, intractable patterns of behavior. These behaviors are usually linked to beliefs that are ingrained and highly resistant to change. They might determine how a person views authority, men's and women's roles, or the nature of children.

When a parent cannot change how he parents and how he communicates with his spouse, it might be that the patterns laid down in his own childhood are so powerful that he cannot modify his view of reality. The clinician might explore a little more closely the parent's own parenting, to give him a perspective on the modeling to which he was exposed. Usually, the couple and I get to this point in the middle of our work, after the couple has been working well for a while and seeming to agree on an approach. At some point, a management tool, such as a point system, breaks down, and a more fundamental disagreement comes to the fore.

I also encounter this problem early on, even before the couple gets to the point of trying and failing at some parenting method. The parents might disagree on issues of strictness and leniency, the roles of fathers and mothers, or who is to blame for the problems that the child is having. These overarching issues permeate the coparenting relationship over and above any particular technique. When couples get stuck in this way, I often ask them how such an issue or problem was handled in their families of origin. Their responses are usually illuminating, and I find that having them talk about it together helps them see that just because things were done that way in their families does not mean they have to be done that way in every family until the end of civilization.

I begin with having the parent who appears to be the most stuck talk about how the matter was handled by his parents. The issues could be, for example, punishment, spanking, time out, communication, and specific behavioral issues such as poor school performance or curfew violations. Following that, I ask the other spouse the same question, and we compare notes to understand how their families of origin influenced their assumptions about parenting. I help them see how they are taking the worldviews of their families of origin and imposing them on their own family. It might help couples to examine these issues a little more systematically and in a little more depth. They might want to list the areas of differences between them and see how they were influenced by their families of origin. They could consider drawing up chart like this and using it as a jumping-off point for discussion:

Issues that have us stuck	How they were handled in Bob's family	How they were handled in Paula's family
Time out vs. spanking		
Length of punishments		
Dinnertime behavior		
Consequences for disrespect		
Praise for good behavior		
Rewards for good behavior		
Number of warnings		
Allowance for chores		
Cleaning up room		

For example, Bob and Paula were trying to eliminate the disrespectful, annoyed tone of voice in which their son Brandon usually addressed them. They were good at correcting him each time he spoke to them in that manner, but it was only Paula who made a point of praising him each time he spoke to them respectfully. Try as he might, Bob could not get used to the idea of praising his son for something he *should* be doing. Although he tried to remind himself to do this, he kept forgetting. Paula was becoming exasperated with him, but her increasingly vocal reminders were not helping.

I asked Bob how good behavior was handled in his family when he was growing up. He remembered that bad behavior was punished but that good behavior was ignored. The children were just expected to behave well and to know what they were supposed to do. Bob added that he believed Brandon did know how to behave respectfully but just would not do it.

I pointed out to Bob and Paula that children with ADHD usually do know the right way to behave, but that they find it difficult to put that knowledge into action when they have to because of their impulsivity. Of course, they *should* behave well, and praising them immediately makes that behavior more likely to occur. If respectful behavior is our goal, this was the way to do it. Further discussion with Bob made him realize that his family of origin was very different from his present family, that there were negative consequences to the way his parents parented, and that he wanted his current family to turn out differently in some respects from his original family.

A couple might benefit from making these comparisons in a more concrete way, examining the pros and cons of the ways each of their families handled things:

Issue that has us stuck	How it was handled in Bob's family	Advantages to handling it this way	Disadvantages to handling it this way

Issue that has us stuck	How it was handled in Paula's family	Advantages to handling it this way	Disadvantages to handling it this way

The couple can then choose which aspects of their families of origin to preserve and which will not work for the family they have created:

Issue that has us stuck	What we want to preserve from Bob's family	What we want to discard from Bob's family	What we want to preserve from Paula's family	What we want to discard from Paula's family

After gaining some insight into their families of origin, Bob and Paula were better able to apply their skills to their own goal, that of improving the disrespectful behavior of their son.

VISITING PARENTS AND RELATIVES WITH THE ADHD CHILD

"Whenever we visit Shawn's grandparents, they just give in to him. They think I'm being ridiculous giving him a time-out. We get home, and his behavior is even more unmanageable." Terry's complaint was an all too common one. If children with ADHD spend a lot of time with their grandparents or other relatives, what should parents do if these family members can't or won't get with the program? What if they actively undermine the parents who are trying to enforce discipline in this new way?

Grandparents and other relatives can be very helpful in reinforcing the parents' authority over the children and in acting in ways that are consistent with the parents' disciplinary methods. Just as often, they can interfere and make it more difficult for the parents to parent when the children are with these family members as well as after the visits have ended. This is especially true if the parents are trying out new disciplinary methods and both they and the other relatives are unfamiliar with them and not accustomed to the parents acting this way. People tend to form set expectations of how other people will behave. If parents act in ways that are, in the eyes of the other person, unusual, he will resist relating to them in an entirely new way, and he will keep pulling them back to the way he is accustomed to.

Many parents with whom I work confidently apply their newly acquired behavior management skills at home, and then feel like they turn into de-skilled, babbling children in front of their parents or in-laws. Parents and in-laws often believe they know much more about raising a child than do the child's parents, and this new-fangled ADHD nonsense is just a fancy way of describing a bratty, spoiled, frustrated, overindulged, or not-indulged-enough (fill in the blank yourself) kid.

So when these parents, who are struggling to make sense of their child's behavior and struggling to be in control of their family, visit their own parents, their parents think that this new behavior on the part of their adult children is strange indeed. They often overtly or covertly blame the parents for the child's behavior anyway, not acknowledging that there could possibly be anything like an inherent disorder. Seeing the unacceptable behavior repeated in their presence and even escalating when the parents do set appropriate limits (after all, it does take more patience to see whether a time-out is effective than to see if a spanking will work), reinforces their belief that it is the parents who are to blame.

Parents eventually have to choose whether it is worth the hassle and disruption to visit their extended family members. The decision not to visit is not one that should be made lightly. It is unreasonable to expect other family members to be perfectly aligned with one's needs, wishes, beliefs, and child-rearing practices. However, it is not unreasonable to expect others to respect one's authority as the parent and one's right to raise his child the way he thinks is best.

Complicating the communication between the parents and grandparents, or other family members, is the unsettling experience that many competent adults have of feeling like small children when they are speaking to, or in the presence of, their own parents. It is as if they enter a strange force field as soon as their parent picks up the phone or as soon as they are within a one-mile radius of their parents' home. All of a sudden, it is impossible to assert oneself in an adult manner, it becomes impossible to set limits and boundaries, one can no longer speak as one would to any other adult or friend. Being with our parents elicits the relationship that they have established with us since we were born, since before we were able to speak. It is a very primitive force that gets triggered emotionally and that, therefore, is beyond logic. It takes a lot of support and practice to do things differently under these circumstances. Asserting oneself in a new way with one's parents is a learned skill that must overcome a lot of past learning.

I usually recommend that prior to the visit the parents inform their own parents or family members of their new approach to managing their child's behavior. They can simply say, "You know we've been having some problems with Johnny's behavior and we're trying to do something about it. We have met with his pediatrician and teacher, and even a child psychologist [it might help for parents to invoke the titles of authorities who back them up—a lot of people are impressed with this, but then again, a lot of people rebel against this as well]. We want you to know that we are trying a new approach, and we want to tell you about it so you won't be surprised or confused and so you'll understand and support what is going on." They then explain what they plan to do if Johnny behaves a certain way, and what they would like their parents to do or refrain from doing. If their parents understand the plan, great! If they do not, the child's parent can say, "Well, you might not understand, but we are asking you to just let us do what we have to do and respect that we have a good reason for doing things that way."

This does not always go smoothly, and each parent has to decide whether it is worth the hassle. I don't think it is realistic to expect that any visit will be hassle-free, and experiencing some hassle is not a good-enough reason not to have contact. Some parents decide to visit but to limit the visits in time or in frequency. Others grin and bear it and pick up the pieces when they get home. There are others who decide that the situation is just too toxic and destructive to their child, and stop visiting or visit seldom. It helps to have a supportive spouse in these situations and to communicate a united front to the grandparents. If one parent feels too undermined, frustrated, or angry to follow through consistently, the other can take over the discipline. If one is unable to communicate effectively and calmly to the grandparents, the other can take over the role of communicator. The parents should also have a plan as to when to leave and how to communicate with each other that it is time. In addition, it is helpful to work out a signal as to when one needs to communicate with one's spouse in private.

Writing down the plan might be helpful for parents:

Our plan for the family visit

What goes wrong at my parents'/relatives' house:

What I need to say to my father/mother/parents/relatives:

When I will say it:______________________________

What I need my spouse to do to support me:

When I will speak to my spouse about it: ____________________

Our plan during the visit:

Our signals to each other:

To talk privately: ____

To leave: ____

What I will do to remain calm:

____

There will be a lot of trial and error in doing this, and parents should not expect perfection. It is important to keep anger and frustration under control, and to concentrate on small successes and victories. This is a learning experience, and after each visit, the parents can review what worked and what did not work, and plan to do things better the next time.

REPARENTING ONESELF

Through some process that I do not completely understand, I have found that when a parent gives his or her children what the parent lacked in his own childhood, the parent can derive a benefit from that parenting similar to the benefit that the child is receiving. By being the kind of parent that one's own parent couldn't be, the parent experiences the benefits of being on the receiving end of that parenting. Nurturing one's child nurtures oneself and can fill in some of what has been missing. For example, a parent who grew up in a chaotic household in which there was much yelling and screaming might experience a profound sense of soothing, safety, and well-being from learning to control his own temper around his children, and knowing that he is creating a calmer, more secure home for his children than his parents created for him.

Ralph, the father of three, struggled with sports as a child. With poor coordination and poor attention skills, he would strike out at bat and commit errors in the outfield in every Little League game. He longed for his father to go out with him to practice, and believed that if he could just get a chance to do that, he would be spared the embarrassment that he experienced at every ballgame. His father was always too busy to make time for this.

When Ralph's children were of school age, Ralph was dreading the prospect of their being interested in sports. "Maybe," he thought, "they won't have any natural ability and they won't be interested."

Ralph was wrong. It wasn't that his children were born athletes, it was that they were born children—they enjoyed running around, playing, and being with other children. They didn't know that sports were things to be afraid of; to them, sports were fun. Ralph decided that, instead of avoiding the issue, he would try to make the sports experience as positive for his children as possible. Instead of just cheering them on and practicing with them, he also tried his hand at coaching. For the first time in his life, by experiencing sports through the eyes of his children, Ralph liked athletics. Ralph nurtured his children's interest in sports, and nurtured their skills as well. He found that what he lacked in experience and knowledge, he made up for in enthusiasm and in his good observational abilities. He was able to point out things his children could do to improve their skills that he could not have done well when he was a child.

Ralph found his own self-confidence as it related to sports improving, even though he was not participating as a player. Creating better players (with his own children) gave him an appreciation of sports that he had never had before, and made him feel a sense of ownership and participation that made sports a part of his identity for the first time in his life.

In giving to his children in this way, Ralph felt given to, himself, replacing to some extent what he had not received from his father. He became a father to himself. Although he was still disappointed in his own father, the resentment he had felt all his life was no longer as strong because he had more of what he needed.

❖ CHAPTER 16 ❖

Final Thoughts

Writing this book helped me to appreciate the many things that clinicians teach parents and help them cope with, often in a brief period of time, when they work with parents of children with ADHD. This guidebook can help clinicians keep track of the important things that they want to convey to parents. Working with ADHD children is complicated, challenging, and rewarding. No two children are the same, and no two parents or sets of parents are the same. The therapeutic relationship that clinicians form with clients is the bedrock of the work, from which all benefit flows. Clinicians must constantly ask themselves if their relationships with clients are therapeutic, whether their boundaries are appropriate, whether they are keeping their needs separate from those of the clients, and whether they are helping the clients define and meet their goals.

Parents of ADHD children must be adequately informed about the disorder, accept its reality, feel clear rather than confused about it, and understand how it applies to their child. Imparting information about ADHD to the parents and addressing their doubts and questions, is an important part of treatment.

This book helps parents consider the question of whether or not their child has ADHD, and helps them understand the process involved in diagnosis and assessment. It is useful to help parents understand the inexactitude of the diagnostic process of ADHD, and the complexities posed by similar and coexisting disorders. Every child with ADHD is unique. Helping the parents to understand their child's problem areas and the situations in which she is vulnerable is essential in helping them achieve competence in coping with them. This guidebook also helps parents identify the goals they want to set in order to resolve specific problems that their child is having. The parents will be helped by brainstorming and then prioritizing what they want to work on, and by coming to terms with their own strengths and weaknesses. Just as they set specific goals for their child's behavior, they can set specific goals for changing their own behavior.

Gaining insight into one's parenting is incomplete without understanding how a parent uses authority. So much of a parent's interaction with a child with ADHD involves authority issues, whether it is giving commands, trying to teach, punishing, praising, setting limits, or maintaining the upper hand in the face of disrespect or control struggles. It is important that parents see they have options and choices in their roles as parents and in how they use authority. Too often, parents become stuck in an inflexible idea of authority that serves to undermine the authority that they seek. The exercises in this book can provide the parents with some insight into their authority styles, and help them develop a greater degree of flexibility.

ADHD children need a lot of skill building. Their impulsivity and inattention prevent them from acquiring skillfulness in many areas important to effective functioning at home, at school, and with peers. The parents of children with ADHD need skill building as well. This book gives parents the opportunity to develop better communication and behavior management skills, to learn about and evaluate the benefits and drawbacks of several different types of behavior management techniques, to tailor the techniques to their own needs, to help their children become more skilled in interacting with others (with the Social Skills Report Card), to understand the effect that attributions have on behavior, and to guide their children toward making more functional attributions. Parents helping their children to structure and prioritize homework and to take responsibility for monitoring their own schoolwork should go a long way to bringing peace to many households. Sequencing skills were also addressed

Many children with ADHD lack an understanding of how other people feel and how they experience the ADHD child's behavior. The process of teaching a child to be empathic was broken down into its component steps in order to help the child develop a richer understanding of other people.

Often, parents feel overwhelmed at the thought of learning something new, when they are struggling so hard with the day-to-day needs of their child. This book teaches how everyday activities, like playing games, eating dinner, and transitioning from one activity to another, can be used as valuable opportunities to teach skills to the ADHD child. Organizing one's physical effects is often a struggle for children with ADHD. Systematic ways to help a child become more organized were reviewed. Since learning to follow rules is often fraught with difficulty, parents can learn to teach their child verbal mediation skills that will help him guide himself according to rules, and to internalize them. It is also important that parents help their children learn to internalize self-soothing skills so they can learn to calm their inner turmoil in order to cope effectively with the world. While we know that internal self-control is important, helping a child control his aggression toward others is also vital to helping him get through life successfully. The messages that parents give their children about aggression need to be carefully thought out and communicated to the child with ADHD.

Since consistency is so important to the child with ADHD, and changes in the environment can be so disruptive, it is important to help the child maintain a mental image of and relationship with a parent who is absent some of the time, such as one who travels on business.

The frustrations of parenting a child with ADHD are complicated by unstated beliefs and feelings about one's child. These thoughts and feelings might be negative, and they get communicated to the child without the parent's even realizing or intending this to happen. Exercises can help the parent be more aware of these underlying thoughts and feelings and have more control over the effect they have on the parent's behavior.

It is hoped that this book has helped parents examine their own and their spouses' strengths and weaknesses, so they can learn from each other and parent more effectively as a team. They have learned what they can change about themselves and what they cannot, and they have this knowledge to help them know when to ask their spouse for help. They have learned to set goals for how they can communicate and parent more effectively and more creatively together, with mutual respect.

Cooperative parenting doesn't end when parents separate or divorce. The child still needs his parents to work together for his benefit, and the work often becomes more difficult. This book has addressed how parents can help their child keep a mental image of the noncustodial parent, cope with the different sets of rules in each household, cope with the transitions from one household to the other with a minimum of behavioral and emotional disruption, deal with confusions about authority, and be kept out of parental conflicts. Parents have also been helped to consider the types of custody arrangements that are best for their child.

The question of medication always comes up for parents of children with ADHD. Many parents have negative feelings and serious fears about putting their child on medication. Addressing these fears empathically, realistically, and productively has been discussed herein.

With all the help and input that parents of ADHD children receive, it is often hard to keep track of what is helping and what is not. Therefore, the parents need to monitor whether or not the input is helping. Methods to assist the parents with this important task were introduced. In addition, we addressed the issue of parents' keeping track of the improvements they have made in their parenting, and whether those are aligned with their goals. Parents were given tools to monitor their behavior and gain insight into their anger. They were also guided in managing the time they spend with their children. They were given assistance in setting goals to learn from each other and help each other to change.

A very poignant moment in working with parents often comes when they begin to consider whether or not they might have ADHD. With this realization come confessions of their own histories of disappointments and missed opportunities. Helping the parents come to terms with this so they can get help rather than avoid it is an important aspect of our work.

Parents were also helped to track their progress and to come to terms with the influences of their own parents on their parenting skills, their self-esteem, and their assumptions about family relationships. We can offer help to free parents from some of the limitations of their histories in order to give them more freedom to parent effectively, as well as to deal more effectively with extended family members in the here and now.

❖ ❖ ❖

References

American Psychiatric Association. (1994). *Diagnostic and Statistical Manual of Mental Disorders*, 4th ed. Washington, DC: American Psychiatric Association.

Barkley, R. A. (1995). *Taking Charge of ADHD*. New York: Guilford.

DuPaul, G. J. (1990). *The Home and School Situations Questionnaires–Revised: Normative Data, Reliability, and Validity*. Unpublished manuscript, University of Massachusetts Medical Center, Worcester, MA.

Jacobs, E. H. (1998). *Fathering the ADHD Child: A Book for Fathers, Mothers, and Professionals*. Northvale, NJ: Jason Aronson.

Tannen, D. (1990). *You Just Don't Understand: Women and Men in Conversation*. New York: Ballantine.

❖ ❖ ❖

Index

ABOUT THE AUTHOR

Edward H. Jacobs, Ph.D., is a psychologist practicing in Londonderry, New Hampshire. He is the founder and director of the Learning Resource Center, where a team of professionals provides evaluations and consultations to children and adults with attention, learning, and behavioral problems. He has served on the clinical faculty and trained as a Clinical Fellow in the Department of Psychiatry, Harvard Medical School. The author of *Fathering the ADHD Child*, Dr. Jacobs writes a parenting column and contributes articles to *The Gazette: The Journal of the Learning Disabilities Association of Massachusetts.* He also writes a biweekly newspaper column. He is a consulting editor of the Book Review Board of the *American Journal of Psychotherapy*. Dr. Jacobs is a member of the staff of Parkland Medical Center in Derry, New Hampshire. A consultant to other therapists, courts, schools, lawyers, and physicians, he has presented numerous workshops and symposia and has appeared on radio and television.